# Once Upon a Time in Rhode Island

by
Katherine Pyle

Illustrated by
Helen B. Mason.

## TO ALL RHODE ISLAND CHILDREN

DEAR GIRLS AND BOYS:

You may be descended from some of the brave men and women whose stories are told in this book, or you may, like them, have come to Rhode Island from across the sea and will some day be citizens of this famous little State.

Whichever you are, these stories are written for you, to show you what kind of men and women laid the foundations of our State; to help you to understand how hard they worked to make it a good place for you to live in, and to make you feel that when you do something fine or brave, you, too, are carrying on the work they began so fearlessly and steadfastly.

So to you, the future citizens of Rhode Island, one of the thirteen original colonies, these true stories of her noble sons and daughters are dedicated.

ESTHER PIERCE METCALF,
ALICE ADAMS JOHNSON,
ELIZABETH BYRON CABOT,
ALICE HALL DURFEE GREENE,
LYRA BROWN NICKERSON,
*for the Society of Colonial Dames in the State of Rhode Island and Providence Plantations.*

# Table of Contents.

|  | PAGE |
|---|---|
| How, Once Upon A Time, As Some People Say, The Norsemen Came To Rhode Island.... | 3 |
| How, Once Upon A Time, Roger Williams Founded A Town In The Wilderness............ | 19 |
| How, Once Upon A Time, The Red Men And The White Men Made War Together......... | 33 |
| How, Once Upon A Time, Rhode Island Gained Her Patent........................ | 53 |
| How, Once Upon A Time, The People Of Rhode Island Destroyed The "Gaspee"........... | 69 |
| How, Once Upon A Time, Newport Learned About War............................. | 85 |
| How, Once Upon A Time, A Rhode Island Man Became The First Admiral Of The American Navy... | 101 |
| How, Once Upon A Time, A Rhode Island Boy Became A Famous General.............. | 117 |
| How, Once Upon A Time, The Battle Of Rhode Island Was Fought................... | 139 |
| How, Once Upon A Time, A Rhode Island Boy Became A Famous Painter............... | 155 |
| How, Once Upon A Time, A Rhode Island Man Became The Hero Of Lake Erie.......... | 173 |
| How, Once Upon A Time, Rhode Island Bore Her Part In The Confederation.............. | 191 |

# INTRODUCTION

This book is published by the Society of Colonial Dames in Rhode Island for the benefit of children in Rhode Island schools, and of Rhode Island children who, though not in school, ought to know and be interested in the early history of the State.

Miss Pyle has not tried to settle the many disputed points in early Rhode Island history, or to make her book in any way a systematic narrative account. Her object has been, rather, to interest her readers in the past by a series of pictures or stories, presented with all possible accuracy in matters of fact, but at the same time in language suited to young people. In such a book, tradition and imagination have their place as well as assured fact, and a story may illuminate a period more effectively than an orderly narrative. Throughout the volume, controverted questions have, for obvious reasons, been avoided so far as possible, and, where they could not be avoided altogether, they have been handled impartially.

I have read Miss Pyle's manuscript carefully, and should not fail to thank the author for the willingness with which she has accepted such suggestions regarding statements of fact or style of treatment as seemed pertinent. The Society at whose charge the volume is issued deserve warm praise for this new proof of their practical interest in Rhode Island history. I bespeak for the book the favorable attention of teachers and parents, and of Rhode Island children, especially the children of foreign birth or parentage, to whom the

## INTRODUCTION

picturesque story of the State is not so familiar as it is to the native-born. If the book awakens new interest in the past, or helps to explain the present, or paves the way for a happier and more useful future, it will have achieved its purpose.

WILLIAM MACDONALD.

*Brown University,*
  *November,* 1914.

How, Once Upon A Time,
As Some People Say,
The Norsemen
Came To
Rhode Island

Tyrker Burst from the Wood

A Viking Ship

IT WAS a bright summer day in the year 985. The wind blew chill from off the shores of Iceland and out to sea. It filled the painted sails of the little dragon-shaped ship that was setting out from the harbor. In the prow of the boat stood the Viking Biarne. His long hair blew about his face. His eyes were as keen and bright as those of a hawk as he looked up at the sails and then out at the open water before him.

He and his men were starting out on a daring expedition. Many of his friends thought it a very foolish one. He was sailing for Greenland, and neither he nor any of the sailors had ever gone that way before. They knew almost nothing of the waters they would have to cross, and in those days there were no maps and charts of the ocean such as we have now. It needed a brave heart to start out on an ocean voyage in those days. But the Vikings were a bold and daring people. They loved the sea and its storms and dangers, and were always ready to set out on adventures. Already other Icelanders, as brave as Biarne, had dared to cross the unknown sea, and had made a settlement in Greenland.

The wind was fair when Biarne and his men set

sail. The little ship plunged boldly on its way. Soon Iceland dropped from sight behind them. Nothing was to be seen but the heaving ocean and the great dome of sky above.

For days the little ship sailed straight on before the wind. It seemed as though the journey to Greenland might be a fair and short one. Then suddenly came a change. A gray fog settled down about the ship. It was like a curtain. The sailors could not see where they were sailing, nor anything around them. The wind now changed round to the north, and began to drive the ship from its course. It rose to a gale that howled around the little vessel. The sails were taken in, but still the gale drove the ship before it, farther and farther to the south. The sailors did not know what dangers they might be driving into. They knew nothing of the great continent that lay to the south of Greenland. They did not even know that the earth was round and had no edge. For all Biarne knew this gale might be driving his ship to the very end of the world, where he might sail over and be lost.

This lasted for days, and then the gale began to die down.

"The wind is changing," said Biarne. "Perhaps now the fog will lift."

And so it did. Once more the sailors could see the sky and the ocean around them. For a day and a night they sailed, not knowing where they were. Then on the second morning a great shout rose among the men. "Land! Land!" they cried. There, off on the horizon, they could see a coastline like a low, blue cloud.

They crowded to the side of the ship, pointing and

wondering. They wondered what land it could be, for they knew they were too far south for it to be Greenland. All this was long before the time of Christopher Columbus and his discovery of America.

Biarne changed the course of his ship, and sailed over as close to the land as he dared to go. It was a low-lying country, with hills and streams and woods and green valleys.

Biarne would not allow his men to land, for he did not know what beasts or wild men might be hidden in the forests; and, besides, the journey had already lasted longer than he had planned. So they sailed away toward the north again, leaving that pleasant coast behind them.

But the story of what they had seen they carried with them to Greenland, and it was a strange tale to the ears of those who were waiting for them there. Little had any of those northern people guessed that a broad and fertile country lay there to the south of them.

It was a story that many listened to and talked about, but none listened more eagerly than a certain man named Lief Ericson.

Lief was a bold and daring man, loving adventure as he loved the breath of life. He was a man to hold to dreams, and to make them come true; and the dream he held to now was that of finding the fair southland and exploring it.

For fifteen years after he heard Biarne's tale he worked and toiled and planned, and at the end of that time he had saved enough money to buy a ship for himself and to hire men to sail it. The ship he bought was no other than the dragon-shaped vessel which had belonged to Biarne.

It was with fair skies and favoring winds that Lief and his comrades set sail at last, and the fine weather was with them through all their voyage down to the southland. In due time they came to the shores that Biarne had told them of, and sailed into a sheltered bay and dropped anchor.[2] It was this harbor where they first anchored that many people have supposed was Mount Hope Bay.

The time of year was early autumn. Nuts were ripening on the trees, and the first leaves were turning red when the Norsemen landed. Besides the nut trees there were fruit trees as well, cherries, mulberries, and plums, though they were now past the time of bearing. There were fish in the streams, and game in the woods, as the Norsemen soon found. It was a land more rich and fertile than they had ever dared to hope to find it.

The band of adventurers at once set about cutting down trees and making a shelter for themselves. As far as Lief could see, he and his men were the only living beings in all the land; but still there might be savages farther inland, and he warned his men to keep watch about the camp, and to have their weapons ready so they could protect themselves at a moment's notice if necessary.

Later on, when they began to explore the country, Lief divided his men into two bands. These bands took turns, one of them going off on expeditions, while the other stayed at home to guard the huts and provisions. The men in each band were told always to keep close together for the sake of safety.

For some time the warning to keep together was carefully followed out, but one day, when the exploring party came back to camp, it was found that

## THE NORSEMEN CAME TO RHODE ISLAND

one of their number was missing; it was a German, Tyrker by name. Lief was greatly troubled. He feared some misfortune had happened to the man. Taking twelve companions with him, he set out in search of the missing one.

The little band had not gone far, however, when they heard a great sound of shouting and holloaing. A moment later Tyrker burst out from the woods nearby. He waved and beckoned, and shouted out some words, but he was so excited that he spoke in German, and the Norsemen could not understand what he was trying to tell them. As he came nearer they saw his mouth and face were smeared with some sort of juice, and his hands were full of luscious looking purple fruit. It was grapes he carried. The Norsemen had never seen any before. Tyrker had found them growing in the woods, and they reminded him so strongly of the vineyards of his own native country that he was wild with joy.

After the Norsemen had tasted the fruit they were almost as delighted with his find as Tyrker was. Lief sent several of them off to gather the bunches and bring them back to the camp. The vines were so loaded down with fruit that not only did the Norsemen have all they could eat of them, but there were enough to dry and store away in the ship to carry home with them.

Lief had, as yet, found no name for the new country, but now he decided to call it *Vinland* on account of the grapes that had been discovered there.

For over a year Lief and his companions stayed in Vinland, hunting, fishing, and exploring. Then in the spring of 1002 they set sail for home, carrying with them a rich cargo of raisins and lumber.

Great was the joy in Greenland over the return of the adventurers, and over the lumber and fruit they had brought with them.

It was not many months after this that Lief's younger brother, Thorwald, made up his mind to see that new country, too. He hired thirty companions, and borrowed his brother's ship, and he, too, set sail one autumn day, as his brother had done before him.

But his voyage was not to prove as peaceful as that of Lief. Misfortune and sorrow were to come upon that little band before the dragon-shaped vessel should return to Greenland.

Thorwald had no trouble in finding the river and the bay that Lief had told him about. Some of his sailors had already been there, and could tell him exactly how to go. They could even tell him where to land, and could point out where Lief had built his "booths," as they called them.

These booths were still standing. The summer storms had scarcely harmed them at all. They were almost exactly as Lief had left them, and Thorwald and his men did not have to build others.

They did a great deal of sailing up and down the coast, for in this way they could go farther than they could possibly have gone on foot. Everywhere there was loneliness, broken only by the sight of a deer, a fox, a lynx, or some other animal, and by the cries of the wild birds. But yet there were other human beings living in that land, as the adventurers were to find before long.

One day Thorwald and his comrades landed on a point of shore with a wooded bluff above it and set about building a fire to cook their noon-day meal. They had not been there long when one of them happened to look up. There, standing on the bluff above, were a number of strange-looking people. They were dressed in the skins of wild animals, and were small and sallow, with ill-formed faces and shaggy hair, and they were armed with bows and arrows.

The man's cry of wonder made his comrades, too, look up, and they felt no little surprise and fear at the sight of the savages.

For a few minutes the two parties stared at each other without moving. Then Thorwald stepped forward, and made motions for the savages to come down and talk with him. Instead of doing this they began to retreat slowly toward the woods behind them. One of the Norsemen, more eager than the rest, started forward to follow them.

At this the savages seemed to become frightened. They turned and fled back to the woods, but before they reached it they stopped to send a flight of arrows down among the strangers.

Thorwald gave a loud cry and sank to the ground. An arrow had pierced his body just below the arm. His followers gathered around him, full of grief and horror, and tried to help him, but they soon saw they could do nothing for him. He was dying.

Thorwald himself knew this. He told them not to move him, but to let him lie there until all was over, and then to bury him where he had fallen.

These last directions were carried out by his followers. His grave was made there in the wilderness, and a rough cross of wood was set up to mark the place. Then, with sad faces and heavy hearts, they went back to the boats, and sailed down to the camps.

With Thorwald's death ended the second settlement in Vinland. His comrades had no longer any wish to stay on in that wild country where death might come to them at any moment. And a few months later they set sail for home.

Many tears were shed in Greenland when the news of Thorwald's death was brought to his people. For years there was no further thought of venturing down to Vinland.

Then in 1007 Thorfinn Karlsefenn (or Thorfinn the Hopeful, as he was called) bought three ships and gathered together 151 men, and made ready to try the adventure.

Now the Norse women of those days were brave and hardy, like the men. Thorfinn had married a strong and daring woman named Gudrum.[3] She loved her husband dearly, and when she heard that he was going to venture down into the country where Thorwald had lost his life she made up her mind to go with him. Six other brave women, the wives of the sailors, declared they, too, would go with their husbands. The men were willing to take them, for they knew how strong and brave their women were.

Great preparations were made for this voyage. The three ships were loaded, not only with food and clothing, but with cattle, seed, tools, and everything that might be needed in going to a new country.

But though Thorfinn and his companions had intended to settle in Vinland, they did not sail directly there. On the way they saw a fine, large bay, and they were so pleased with the appearance of it that they decided to land there and settle for the winter. But it was a hard winter for the voyagers. Instead of the mild, open weather they had hoped for, it was bitterly cold, with ice and snow and sleet. The streams were frozen so hard that they could not fish;

# THE NORSEMEN CAME TO RHODE ISLAND

game was scarce; before the winter was over almost all their provisions had been used.

One day a dead whale was washed up on the shore of the bay. There was great rejoicing when this was found. It was enough to last for weeks. They cut great slices from it, and cooked them over the fire, and part of it they dried and stowed away for use later on.

It was in the very midst of the coldest weather that a little baby was born to Gudrum. Snovu they named it, for that is a good Norse name. This, as far as we know, was the first white child born in America.

In the spring, as soon as the weather permitted, Thorfinn and his people sailed to Vinland. They hoped to find it milder and more sheltered there, as indeed it proved to be.

Lief's booths were still standing, though the storms had partly destroyed them, so that they were of little use except to show where he had camped. It was necessary to build new ones and also to make an enclosure where the cattle could be kept.

One day, when the settlers were busily at work, they were startled to see a band of savages appear from a wood nearby. The voyagers made haste to seize their weapons and make ready to defend themselves, but the savages made signs that there should be peace between them and the strangers. They had brought some dried fish and fruit, furs and skins of wild animals, that they wished to trade for tools and seeds. The Norsemen were very willing to do this, for they had more than enough of their own things, and what the savages brought would be very useful to them. After this there was much trading between the white men and the natives; "Skraelings" the Norsemen called them. The settlers grew quite used to seeing them around, and no longer dreamed of any danger from them. But danger there was, and they would have done well to guard against it.

Among the cattle that the Norsemen had brought with them there was a bull that was very wild and fierce. One day this bull broke out of the enclosure and rushed away toward the forest, bellowing as it went. A number of the Norsemen ran after it, shouting, and trying to turn it back.

It happened that a band of Skraelings was on the way to the camp at that very time. Suddenly the bull came charging through the woods toward them, with the Norsemen close behind it. The savages thought it was an attack, and they fled away, full of terror.

For a whole month the Norsemen saw nothing more of them. They wondered what had become of them and why they no longer came to the booths. They never dreamed that the Skraelings were angry and were planning revenge.

Then one morning, while the Norsemen were quietly going about their business, a flight of arrows sang about them. One man fell, shot through the head. Others of the Norsemen were wounded. Those who were unhurt ran to their booths, caught up their weapons, and returned the attack so fiercely that the savages fled, leaving several dead and wounded behind them.

After this attack Thorfinn felt it would no longer be safe for him and his companions to remain in Vinland. There was no telling when the Skraelings might again return and try to avenge themselves,

# THE NORSEMEN CAME TO RHODE ISLAND

so goods and cattle were gathered together, the ships were loaded as quickly as possible, and the adventurers set sail again for Greenland.

Thus ended the third and most important settlement the Norsemen ever made in Vinland. For a few years after this other Norsemen came at times, but they came principally to get lumber, which was of great value to them. But after the year 1350 we hear no more even of these expeditions. For centuries Vinland was left wild and undisturbed. The savages roamed there at will, untroubled by the presence of any white man.

In 1524 an Italian named Verrazzano sailed into Narragansett Bay and explored it. A hundred years later a Dutchman, Adrian Block, visited it, and Block Island was named for him; but neither of these men did more than land on the shore for a short time. It was not until Roger Williams and his companions came there in 1636 that the land was really settled; and this was more than six centuries after Biarne's ship was blown down toward our shores on its way from Iceland to Greenland.

The Old Stone Mill

## NOTES

1. There has been much discussion as to whether the Norsemen were the first to discover our New England shores. The Icelandic sagas give detailed accounts of voyages made by Biarne and others which might seem to indicate that Vinland, where the Norsemen settled, was somewhere in Rhode Island. It was long thought that the old Stone Mill at Newport was built by them, but such was not the case. The Norsemen were Christians, and Professor Rafn suggested that it might have been built as a Christian baptistery.

2. On his way north Biarne sighted two other places which may have been Nova Scotia and Newfoundland.

3. Sometimes given as Gudrid; she was the widow of Thorwald.

It Must Have Been a Strange Sight to See Williams in His Neat Black Suit Among the Half-naked Savages

# How, Once Upon A Time, Roger Williams Founded A Town In The Wilderness

Roger Williams Leaves Salem

IT WAS a bleak, cold day in February of the year 1631. An English vessel was slowly making its way up the Boston Harbor. On the deck stood a little group of people, all eagerly watching the strange, wild shore they were coming to. These people had come out from England to join the colonists who had already settled in New England. Puritans the most of them were, and many of them had been persecuted at home because of their religious beliefs. But in this new country they hoped to find liberty and the freedom to worship God as they pleased.

Among those who landed when the ship at last cast anchor were the young clergyman, Roger Williams, and his wife. Roger Williams was already known to many of the New England Puritans. They had heard of him as "a godly minister." They were well pleased that he had come out to join their colony, and they gave him a warm welcome.

Very soon after Williams reached New England he was asked to become a minister in the Salem church. He accepted, but remained only a short time. The Boston church had never entirely separated from the Church of England, but Williams himself had left the English Church.

In Salem he busied himself with teaching and preaching, and also began to seek out the Indians and make friends with them.

Even before he had left England, Williams had heard a great deal about the American Indians and the miserable way they lived, knowing little or nothing about God or religion. His heart was filled with pity for them, and he longed to help and teach them. He felt that in many ways they were treated unjustly by the white settlers who had come among them.

Williams often declared that the Indians were the only real owners of all the land in America, and that they were the only ones who had any right to give it away or sell it.

These ideas were a great offence to the Puritans. What land they held had been made over to them by the King of England. He had given them a paper called a charter, and in it had granted them the land. It seemed almost like treason to say the king had had no right to do this, that it all belonged to the heathen savages.

The colonists, indeed, had neither respect nor love for the Indians. They feared them almost more than they despised them. Terrible tales were told in the settlements of Indian uprisings and massacres; of how this or that settler had suddenly disappeared, and afterward been found lying dead, pierced through by an Indian arrow or scalped by an Indian tomahawk. Many a stormy night the more timid of the colonists must have lain awake, fancying they heard the terrible war-whoop of the Indians in the whistling of the wind, or that the raindrops were the sound of Indian moccasins.

But Williams paid little or no attention to these stories. He felt no fear of the savages. Often, in spite of all his wife could say to prevent him, he would start off alone for the Indian villages. There he would spend days at a time living in their wigwams, eating their food, and sleeping on the heaps of skins or mats that were their beds, and talking to them of God and religion. His whole desire was to do them good, though perhaps they understood but little of what he told them.

Many of the Indians knew some English, but Williams felt he could do more for them if he were able to speak their language. He therefore set himself to learn it, though it was a hard and difficult task. They had no alphabet; they had no books. They could not spell their words for him. All he could do was to listen to their strange guttural speech, and try to repeat the sounds, and understand what they meant.[1]

He intended, later on, when he knew more about them, to write a book on their ways and customs, so that other white men could learn about them and perhaps help them.

The New England Indians all belonged to the large, general tribe of Algonquins; but this was divided into a number of smaller tribes. Of these the Narragansetts were the most friendly and the Pequots the most cruel and treacherous. It was oftenest in the wigwams of the Narragansetts that Williams stayed. Their great chief Canonicus became his close friend, though, as we are told, that great sachem was "most shy" with all other Englishmen.

It must have been a strange sight to see Williams

in his neat black suit, his white cuffs and collar, his high, stiff hat, and buckled shoes sitting there among the half-naked savages. In warm weather the Indians wore little but a piece of deerskin, a belt, and moccasins. Often their faces were painted, and they wore feathers stuck in their coarse black hair. Around their necks hung necklaces made of the claws of animals strung together, or pieces of copper, or beads.

Their wigwams, in which Roger Williams spent so many days, were made of poles fastened together near the top and covered with mats or bark. A hole was left in the top as a sort of chimney, and the fire was built directly under it. On wet or windy days the smoke was apt to be driven back into the wigwams, so that the eyes stung and watered with it and it was hard to breathe. "Filthy, smoky holes," Williams called them, but the discomfort and the filth never kept him from going there.

When he came back to the town he would again take up his disputes with the Puritans, and wrote long letters to protest against their conduct, or to explain his own. The Puritans grew more and more dissatisfied with him and his opinions.[2] He disagreed with them in almost all their ideas about the church and government; and when he disagreed with them he never hesitated to tell them so, nor to tell others, either. The disputes between them grew into quarrels, and the quarrels became more bitter every day.[3]

Moreover, the Puritan rulers in Boston allowed the magistrates there to punish people not only for breaking the laws about lying and stealing, and so on; they also had the right to punish people for not going to church, or for breaking the Sabbath day, or for not believing as the Puritan ministers taught them. This seemed to Williams very wrong. He did not think the magistrates should have any such power as that.

Before long the General Court at Boston ordered the Salem church to dismiss him, and he went to live at Plymouth for a time. Later on, however, he again returned to Salem. The most of his friends were there, and those who believed in his teachings and had become his followers. He now separated himself from the church entirely. He would not even pray with his wife because she still went to church and was a member of it.

It seemed to the Puritans that there would never be any peace in the colony as long as Roger Williams was there. He did nothing, so it seemed to them, but disturb people and stir them up against the rulers. They decided that he must leave and go elsewhere, where, they did not care; back to England, or into the wilderness, or perhaps down to the Dutch colony of New Netherland, only he must go. An order to leave the New England colonies within six weeks was sent him in October of the year 1635.[4]

But at the time this order reached Roger Williams he was ill, too ill to travel. On this account the General Court of Boston gave him permission to stay in Salem until the following spring, but it forbade him, during that time, to preach, or to speak to the people in any public place. But the General Court did not forbid him to talk with his friends at home.

People began to gather about him in his house, sometimes as many as a dozen at a time, to hear him talk. Many of these became his followers.

It was not long, however, before the news of this came to the ears of the Puritan rulers. They were told how Williams was still teaching his dangerous ideas to the people. They began to regret bitterly that they had allowed him to remain in Salem. They also began to lay plans as to how they could get rid of him without waiting until spring.

A vessel was sailing for England early in January, and it was secretly arranged by the General Court that Williams should be put aboard this vessel and sent back to England. If only they could once get him out of the colony the rulers would see to it that he never set foot within their boundaries again.

It was only three days before the ship was to sail that Williams learned of the plot against him. At once, and without waiting an hour, he gathered together some of his belongings, and prepared to set out into the wilderness to seek a refuge there.

It was the dead of winter and bitterly cold. A heavy snow lay on the ground. Only one companion went with him. This was his faithful servant, Thomas Angell; Mistress Williams could not have left her children, nor could she have borne the hardships and exposure of her husband's long wanderings.

For fourteen weeks Williams and Angell wandered from place to place. Sometimes they journeyed on foot, breaking their way through the snowdrifts; sometimes they paddled along the shore in canoes.[5] Their only shelter was in the wigwams of the savages. They were not only half frozen, but almost starved as well. The streams were frozen and game was scarce. Williams afterward spoke of how, through those fourteen weeks of suffering, he had not known "what bread or bed did mean."

Toward spring things grew somewhat better. It was not so bitterly cold, and it seemed more possible to get food.

Williams knew that it would not be safe for him to try to return to Massachusetts. He determined to make a home for himself in the wilderness, where there would be none to trouble him and where he could have his wife and children with him. It would be no cross to him to have none but Indians around him. He wrote that his soul's desire was "to do the natives good," and "not to be troubled with English company."

The place where he at last decided to build a house was a piece of ground on the east side of the Seekonk River, probably somewhere in the present town of Rehoboth.

Several of his friends came out to join him there, though not, as he declared, because of any urging from him. "Out of pity," he wrote, "I gave leave to Mr. Harris, then poor and destitute, to come along in my company, I consented to John Smith, miller at Dorchester (banished also), to go with me . . . to a poor young fellow, Francis Wicks, as also to a lad of Richard Waterman's." Besides the four he named, Joshua Verrin came also.

It was now April. The streams were running clear. The ground was softening. Hopefully this little band of pioneers set about getting lumber for their homes, laying out gardens, and breaking ground for crops. No other white men were within sound or reach.

All about them were the Indians, but they were so friendly that the settlers had no fear of them. There seemed, indeed, nothing to interfere with the success of the new settlement. Already Williams was planning for the time when he could send for his wife and children to come out and join him.

But suddenly, in the midst of all the planning and building, a letter was brought to Williams. It came from Governor Winslow at Plymouth, and it was written to tell Williams that the place he had chosen for a settlement was within the borders of the Plymouth Colony.

The colony owned all the land on the east side of the river, and Winslow regretfully wrote that Williams and his friends would not be allowed to stay there.

This was heavy news for the settlers. Already their houses were partly built. The ground was broken and a part of their seed had been sown. But hard as it was to leave this spot they had chosen, they did not dare to disobey the orders of the Governor. The very day the letter came they began to make their preparations to leave. Provisions were gathered together, axes and tools were brought from the houses where they had been in use, clothes and bedding were rolled up and fastened in bundles.

It would be necessary to cross the river before they could get beyond the borders of the Plymouth Colony. They had only one canoe, and when it was loaded, and they had started out on the river in it, they were in great danger of being swamped. Slowly and carefully they paddled out into the stream and toward the opposite shore. At the point they were making for a great rock, afterward called "Slate Rock," overhung the water. Suddenly upon this rock, dark against the sky, appeared the figures of several Indians. For a few moments they stood watching with interest the loaded canoe. Then across the water they called a friendly greeting: "What Cheer, Netop?"

Williams answered them with like friendliness, and, as the canoe drew in toward shore, the natives came down to meet him. Williams began to talk to them in the Indian language, and presently he learned that all this land on the west side of the river belonged to Canonicus and his tribe. No white man had any right to any part of it. This was good news for Williams, for Canonicus was still his close and trusted friend, and would grudge him nothing.

Cheered by the knowledge they had gained, the white men again pushed their canoe out into the stream and took up their journey. As they went they watched the shore for a promising spot to land.

They paddled around the headlands now known as India and Fox Points, and into the Mooshassock River. Here they came upon a place where three streams met.

The land rose from the water in a gentle slope, and a spring, crystal clear, bubbled up not far from the shore. It would scarcely have been possible to find a better place for a settlement.

They landed, and found a number of Indians had already encamped there, and were cooking their evening meal. This spot was indeed quite close to the Pequot Path, which was the principal highway for the Indians when they journeyed around Narragansett Bay, and on toward the south.

The natives welcomed the white men among them, and gave them a share of the boiled bass and succotash they had just prepared. These Indians assured the white men that if they chose to settle here they might do so in peace. None would hinder them and none would grudge them the land, least of all Williams's good friend Canonicus. "It is God's good providence that has brought us safely to this spot," cried Williams with deep thankfulness, and he determined to make here a settlement that should be a place of refuge for all who were persecuted or "distressed for conscience sake" as he had been. And it was in remembrance of God's great mercies to him that he gave to his first settlement in Rhode Island the name of *Providence.*

What Cheer, Netop

# NOTES

1. Two Indian words may perhaps serve to show how difficult was the task that Williams undertook. "Nooroomantammoonkanunonnash" means "our loves," ánd "Kummogkodonattoottummooetiteaongannunnonash" means "our question."

2. Williams had already drawn down on himself the disapprobation of the Boston church, and the General Court at Boston remonstrated with the church of Salem for admitting him to the ministry there.

3. The principal causes of offence that Williams gave to the Puritan rulers seem to have been:
*First.* "His violent and tumultuous carriage against the patent," meaning the charter given them by the king.
*Second.* For his opinion that "a magistrate ought not to tender an oath to an unregenerate man, for that we thereby have communion with a wicked man in the worship of God, and cause him to take the name of God in vain."
*Third.* "The heavy and turbulent spirit" of his letters to the Puritan rulers.
*Fourth.* His separation of himself from all the churches in the country.

4. This order read, "Whereas Mr. Roger Williams, one of the elders of the church of Salem, hath broached and divulged new and dangerous opinions against the authority of magistrates; has also writ letters of defamation, both of magistrates and churches here, and that before any conviction, and yet maintained the same without any retraction; it is therefore ordered that the said Mr. Williams shall depart out of this jurisdiction within six weeks now next ensuing, which, if he neglect to perform, it shall be lawful for the Governor and two of the magistrates to send him to some place out of this jurisdiction, not to return any more without license from the Court."

5. Mr. Strauss, in his book on Roger Williams, writes: "According to the weight of authority . . . when Williams left Salem he made his way from there by sea, coasting probably from place to place during the 'fourteen weeks,' . . . and holding intercourse with the native tribes."

The English Shot Them Down as They Ran

ID, Once Upon A Time,
The Red Men And The
White Made War
Together

It Was a Bitter Thing for Philip to Have to Do

OF ALL the Indian wars in New England, King Philip's War was the bloodiest and most cruel.

King Philip[1] was the king of the Wampanoag Indians. His father, Massasoit, had been one of the greatest of all the Indian sachems. He and his tribe had owned all the land where Bristol now stands, and from there north, around Mount Hope Bay, and south as far as Sakonnet.

But before Massasoit died, and Philip became chief, much of this land had passed into the possession of the white men. They had bought it from the Indians for a few coats, or tools, or firearms, or strings of wampum. They had divided it into fields, and fenced it about, and built towns. The Indians who had once fished in its streams, and hunted in its woods, no longer had any right to it. They were being driven out by the white men. Not only their land, but their former liberty, too, was being taken from them, for the English made laws, and the Indians who broke them were punished.

When King Philip looked about him and saw all this, his heart grew bitter within him. He longed to bring back power and freedom to his tribe, and to drive the white men from the land they had taken.

But one tribe alone could never do this. The English were very powerful. They had firearms and ammunition. Many native tribes must band together before they would be strong enough to war against the white men.

And so Philip began secretly to send out his messengers to other tribes to tell them of their wrongs and of all that the English had done to them, and to urge them to join with his people and rise against the white men.

But secretly as Philip worked, some news of what he was doing leaked out and became known among the colonists. The rumors caused the English great anxiety, for of all the dangers of this wild land none was so feared as an uprising of the Indians, and a massacre.

Many of the more timid of the English, and those who lived in lonely settlements, left their houses and took refuge in the towns or in fortified places. Settlers armed themselves and took precautions to guard their women and their children. Even when they went to church they carried their loaded firearms with them.

The anxiety grew so great that Governor Prince of Plymouth, and some of the Massachusetts rulers, decided to hold a meeting in the meeting-house in Taunton. Philip was ordered to appear before this meeting and answer the charges that had been made against him — charges that he was arming his warriors, and that he was stirring up other Indians to rise against the white men.

Philip was very unwilling to obey this summons. He sent back a proud answer. "The Governor of Massachusetts is only a subject," he said. "I am a king. I will not treat unless my brother king, Charles of England, is here."

Another and more threatening order was sent, and this time Philip dared not disobey. He went to Taunton, but he took with him seventy of his bravest warriors, and all were armed. King Philip himself was very magnificent. Over his clothes he wore a scarlet blanket. A wonderful belt of wampum was wound about him. It was nine inches wide, and wrought with strange figures of birds and beasts and flowers, and it was fringed with red hair. Around his neck was another band of wampum, with a star hanging from it. His headpiece was also of wampum; it was trimmed with feathers, and so long it hung far down his back.

When he reached Taunton and found that the meeting was to be held in a building, and that he was expected to go in and talk with the English shut in by walls, he at first refused. Only after it had been arranged that the white men should all keep on one side of the meeting-house, and the Indians on the other, would he enter the building.

The Puritan rulers were stern, keen men. Philip, too, was keen; but when he found how much the white men knew about his plotting — that they even knew he had planned to attack Taunton — he could hardly tell how to answer them. He was afraid to confess that all they said of him was true, and yet he dared not quite deny it, either.

In the end the Governor and commissioners refused to allow Philip to leave the town until he had signed a treaty of peace with them. This was a hard thing for Philip to have to do, for by this treaty it was agreed that all his warriors should hand over their arms to the white men. This meant that all his plans for a war were destroyed, for a time at least. Without arms his warriors could do nothing, and it would be a long time before they could again collect enough guns and ammunition to fight the English.

When the Wampanoags returned to Mount Hope their hearts were black with rage. They once more began their secret plotting and planning, but the white men were now watchful and fearful. It was hard for the natives to get hold of any sort of weapons. Few or none among the white traders would now sell firearms to an Indian.

Colonel Benjamin Church was an officer well known throughout New England. He was well known not only to the white men, but to the Indians as well. The natives felt a great respect for him because he understood their ways, and was not afraid to venture among them.

It was a custom among the Indians to hold a dance before they decided any matter that was of great importance.

Early in the summer of 1675 Awashonks, the squaw sachem (that is the queen) of the Sogkonate Indians, sent word to Church that she was holding a dance, and wished him to come to it.

Colonel Church was more than eager to go. He hoped that if he went to the dance he might learn something of what the Indians intended toward the white men. He started out on horseback the very day the message reached him, taking with him only a young lad who understood the Indian language.

When they reached the Sogkonate's country they found the dance had already begun. Awashonks herself, all "in a foaming sweat," was leading it.

As soon as she saw Church, she left the dance and seated herself to talk to him, while her chief men gathered about her.

Awashonks told the colonel that Philip had sent messengers to her to tell her the English were gathering together a great army, and intended to come out into the Indian country and attack them. Philip had urged her to join with his tribe in a war against the white men, and she wished to know what Colonel Church thought about it.

Colonel Church told her that he had just come from Plymouth; that no army was gathering there, and as far as he knew there was no talk of a war. He then asked to see the messengers that Philip had sent.

Awashonks called them, and the Mount Hope men came forward. There were six of them. They were fierce and cruel-looking Indians. Their faces were painted with bright colors, and their hair trimmed up in a comb shape. On their backs were powder-horns and shot-bags.

Church stepped forward and felt the bags, and found they were full of bullets. "What are these for?" he asked.

"To shoot pigeons," answered the braves scornfully.

Colonel Church then told the messengers they were bloody wretches, who thirsted after the lives of their English neighbors, and he advised Awashonks to have them killed, and shelter herself with the English.

When the Wampanoags heard this they were filled with fury, and would have killed Church if they could, but Awashonks' men prevented them. The colonel then again urged her to do nothing against the English. He said that if she took part in any war against them she and her tribe would surely be destroyed, but if she kept the peace the white men would see that no harm came to her.

Awashonks thanked him for his advice, and told him she would think it over, and then she sent him home with two of her men to protect him on the way. And in fact she never did join with Philip.

Church soon afterward talked with Peter Nummit, who was the husband of the queen of the Pocassets, and Peter told him that there would certainly be a war. Philip had held a great war dance the week before, and Indians from many different tribes had come to it.

This news added to the alarm of the English. Companies were formed and officers appointed. Many places were fortified and supplied with arms and ammunition. Roger Williams, now an old man, was asked to take command of a company of Providence militia. This he did, and by his advice several of the buildings were fortified.

Again Philip was sent for to come to Plymouth and answer to the charges against him. This time he came willingly enough, but the rulers could prove nothing against him, and were obliged to allow him to return to Mount Hope.

The great anxiety was lest the Narragansetts,[2] too, should join with Philip's forces, for the Narragansetts were a great and powerful tribe. As long as they could be kept quiet the danger was not so desperate, but if they, too, started on the warpath it might end in a massacre of all the English.

In June the Governor and Assistants at Boston de-

## RED MEN AND THE WHITE MADE WAR

termined to send commissioners to the Narragansetts to urge them to keep peace. Williams was asked to go with them and use his influence with the Indians. He was quite willing to go, but he had small hope of doing any good. He was now old and poor. He could no longer carry with him gifts to win the Indians' good-will. His wise friend Canonicus was dead, and the young warriors cared little for his advice.

When he reached their village he was well received. The warriors sat with him and listened with grave attention to all he had to say; they even made him many good promises, but Williams felt that their fair words and promises meant little. They would break them as soon as it suited them, and he returned home heavy-hearted and full of anxious fears.

It was on Sunday, the 24th of June, 1675, that the first shots of the war were fired, and they were fired by the white settlers and not the Indians. The first man killed was a Wampanoag.

Philip's wise men had told him that whichever side shed the first blood would be defeated.[3] Philip believed this, and until that June Sunday he would not allow any one of his warriors to kill man, woman, or child of the English. He allowed them to burn and plunder as they chose, but not until an Indian had first been killed might they begin their massacre.

On that June day all was peaceful and sunny and quiet in the little settlement of Swansea. The settlers had gone to church, taking their wives and children with them. The houses lay deserted. In the barnyards the chickens scratched and clucked; the cows were peacefully chewing the cud, and the horses stood resting and flicking away flies. Over everything lay the sunny Sabbath day silence.

Suddenly, and as silently as shadows, a band of Indians appeared before one of the houses. They had discovered that it was unprotected, and had come to burn and destroy. They set fire to the buildings, and then began to kill the animals. They were in the midst of this work when the settlers returned. The people of the village had seen the smoke in the distance as they came from church. They came rushing home, full of rage and horror, and tried to drive the Indians away. The Indians resisted, and in the struggle that followed one of them was shot. The others fled, but they were now free to take revenge in any way they chose, for the first blood of the war had been shed, and it was the English who had shed it.

The next day the Indians returned to Swansea and killed several settlers. Almost at once other towns and settlements were attacked. Brookfield in Massachusetts was burned. Hadley, Deerfield, Northfield, Springfield, all were attacked. Many of the inhabitants fled to Newport or Portsmouth for shelter  The people of Warwick also sought refuge on the island, leaving their town deserted. Everywhere was fear, panic, and horror.

Four days after the massacre of Swansea, troops under the command of Major Savage marched to Mount Hope. They hoped to find Philip there, but he and all his men had disappeared. The soldiers found only the ashes of their campfires, and the heads and hands of the murdered white men stuck on poles.

Colonel Church afterward tracked the Mount

Hope sachem to Pocasset, but once again Philip escaped, this time into Massachusetts. It seemed, indeed, almost impossible ever to know where the Indians were, or which place would be the next one to suffer. Suddenly they would gather, a settlement would be attacked, and then, before troops could arrive, the savages would disappear again as suddenly and mysteriously as they had come. Only now and then were they overtaken and forced into an open fight.

The white men, on their side, destroyed a number of Indian villages. They set fire to the wigwams, and those of the Indians who escaped from the flames were killed by the white men's knives or bullets. The English spared none of them, neither old nor young, women nor children, nor the helpless babies. Some of the younger and stronger Indians, however, were saved alive and sold as slaves.

In November the English openly declared war against the Indians, and a reward was offered for Philip, alive or dead. But no one knew what had become of him. Some said he had taken refuge in Canada for the winter; some that he had gone to New Netherland (New York); others believed the Narragansetts were sheltering him in their fort in the Great Swamp.

This swamp was a lonely and dismal place near the centre of what is now South Kingstown. The trees there grew so thickly that their branches made it dark in the swamp even at noonday. The ground was so soft and treacherous it was impossible to cross it except by a secret path of logs that the Indians had made.

In the middle of this swamp was a piece of solid

ground, and upon this the Indians had built their fort. The only way to get to it was by the path of logs.

The fort covered three or four acres of ground, and was made of logs and brushwood.[4] One place in the wall at the northeast corner was still unfinished, and across this the Indians laid a log for protection. Inside the fort was a village of about five hundred wigwams and some roughly built houses.

Here the Narragansetts had stored all the provisions they had gathered for the winter, the grain, the dried meat and fish and acorns that were to last them through the long, frozen months, and were all they would have to live on.

When the fighting first began the Wampanoags sent many of their women and children to the Narragansetts for shelter. It was suspected by the English that the Narragansetts were giving shelter and help to Wampanoag warriors as well, though they could not prove it.

Canonchet was at this time the chief of the Narragansetts.

In November Governor Winslow of Plymouth sent a message to Canonchet ordering him to give up all the Wampanoags who had taken shelter with him. This he must do to prove to the white men that he was keeping faith and not dealing treacherously with them. Not long before, Canonchet and his principal men had signed a treaty of peace with the English. He knew the power of the white men, and he feared it, but still he would not give up those who had come to him for refuge.

He sent back to Governor Winslow a bold and haughty answer. "Not a Wampanoag nor the nail of a Wampanoag" should be given up to the English.

The Puritan rulers had for some time suspected that the Narragansetts were not keeping to their treaty of peace. They suspected that they were aiding the Wampanoags in many ways: even that some of the Narragansett warriors had fought with Philip's men. When this bold answer was received the rulers determined to send troops into Rhode Island and attack Canonchet in his fort.

A large force of soldiers and militia was gathered together under the command of Governor Winslow. There were 550 of the Massachusetts troops, 315 from Connecticut, and 158 from Plymouth. Besides these there were several Rhode Island sailors who had volunteered, and about 120 friendly Indians.

Rhode Island, as a colony, would gladly have sent her share of the troops, but this the Puritan leaders would not allow. Many Jews and Quakers, as well as others who differed from the Puritans, had been allowed to settle in Rhode Island. Here they lived in peace, worshipping God as they pleased. Williams himself did not belong to any church. The Puritans called Rhode Island a colony of heretics, and they would not allow heretics to be their companions, even in a war against the savages.

The troops that were to attack the fort gathered in the town of Wickford, about fifteen miles from the Great Swamp. It was near midnight of the 19th of December when they set out. The weather that winter was bitterly cold. Everything was frozen hard. Even the Great Swamp itself was turned to solid ground. A heavy snowstorm was raging. The soldiers were almost blinded by the flakes. Their hands grew so numb they could hardly hold their guns. Often they stumbled and almost fell in the drifts that grew deeper every hour.

It was not until one o'clock of the next day that they reached the edge of the swamp. By that time they were almost exhausted, and a halt was called.

An Indian deserter from the fort had been captured near the swamp, and from him General Winslow learned the plan of the fort, and also the fact that there was an opening at the northeast corner. It was at that point he planned to make his attack, but he would give his troops time to rest before going farther.

The soldiers stood there at rest, trying to warm their numbed fingers, and staring curiously about them.

Suddenly from behind trees and fallen logs a volley of bullets and arrows was poured into their midst. Many a poor fellow dropped where he stood, staining the snow with his blood. A band of Indians had been hidden in this part of the wood and had been waiting to attack the English in case they tried to enter here.

As the men heard the cries and groans of their wounded comrades all weariness was forgotten. They were filled with fury, and seizing their weapons they charged into the forest. The Indians fled before them, but the soldiers followed close after them up to the very walls of the fort, firing as they ran. They had scarcely reached the fort, however, when the Indians within poured out such a fierce fire of shots that the troops fell on their faces in the snow, and lay there until they could crawl back to the shelter of the trees.

But they were not discouraged. Fresh troops came up to reinforce them, and a second and more desperate attack was made. It carried them under and over the log that blocked the gap, and into the fort.

Here the fight raged even more fiercely. Many of the Indians took shelter in the log houses, and fired from there. The troops were driven back toward the wall, and the fierce war-whoops of the Indians rose in triumph. But suddenly their whoops were changed to cries of dismay. The Connecticut troops had circled the fort and entered from the other side where it was unprotected. Now they were firing on the savages from the rear.

The Indians were ill-prepared for this fresh attack. They had already used almost all of their bullets and powder. Even their arrows were almost gone. Many of them now tried to escape out of the fort into the forest, but they were shot down by the white men as they ran, or knocked in the head by the troops outside. The dusk was falling, but through the twilight still sounded the fierce cries of those who fought, volleys of shot, and the groans of the wounded.

Suddenly the air was reddened by a strange glow. It wavered and sank, and then blazed up brighter. Some one had set fire to the wigwams. The wind was blowing a gale, and the flames leaped from one wigwam to another. The log houses, too, caught fire. Soon the whole village was blazing. Dark figures burst out through the burning walls of the dwellings and ran across the open. Many of them were squaws carrying babies in their arms, or dragging little children by the hands. They could be clearly seen against the snow, and the English shot them down as they ran. No mercy was shown to any one. A number of wounded men were still in the wigwams, and could not escape, and their cries rose above the roaring of the flames.

For a time the whole swamp seemed filled with horror. Then as the flames slowly died down the volleys of shot, too, died out. Those of the Indians who had not been killed or taken prisoners had escaped into the forest. Silence fell over the fort, broken only by the commands of the officers, a low word among the men, or the moaning of the wounded.

The English had won. The victory was theirs, but they had paid a heavy price for it. Many of their officers and men lay dead in the snow. Still more were desperately wounded. Those who were unhurt were faint and exhausted by the march and the fighting. In spite of their condition, however, the officers determined to return at once to Wickford. They were afraid to stay in the fort. They did not know what fresh bands of savages might be gathering about them in the darkness. They had no food for their men, either. The provisions belonging to the Indians, and which they might have used, had been burned in the wigwams.

That journey back to their camp was a terrible one for the troops. More men died on the way back, it was reckoned, than had been killed at the fort.[5]

After the white men had left the swamp the Indians who were still alive crept back to the smouldering ruins of their village. Here they tried to find a little food and warmth. As Canonchet looked about him and saw how few were left, his heart was filled with grief and rage. He now cared for nothing but revenge.

That winter many of his people died of starvation, but when the spring came the remnant started on the warpath. A few Wampanoags joined them, but their tribe, too, was scattered. Many settlements and towns were attacked by these remaining warriors, however. Once more houses were burned and people massacred.

In March a band of soldiers under Captain Michael Pierce set out for Study Hill, in Cumberland. They had learned that Canonchet and his men had a camp there, and they hoped to surprise them and force them to surrender. The soldiers were themselves, however, surprised in a ravine and massacred. Not more than two or three of them escaped alive.

The Narragansetts were filled with triumph over this massacre. Soon afterward they attacked the town of Rehoboth, and Providence itself was attacked, fifty-four houses burned, and many people killed.

It is said that when Williams heard the Indians were coming to Providence he went to meet them alone and unarmed, and urged and entreated them to spare the town. He warned them of the punishment that would surely come to them if they carried out their plans.

But the Indians would not listen to him. "Let the English come," they said; "we will meet them." Then they added, "But you, Brother Williams, you are a good man. You have been kind to us many years. Not a hair of your head shall be touched."

And this promise was kept. In the midst of the destruction that followed no harm came to Williams or to any one belonging to him.

But this attack on Providence was the last of

Canonchet's victories. Soon after he was taken prisoner, and on April 3, 1676, he was shot. He had been offered his life if he would promise to make his people submit to the English, but this he refused to do. He was not afraid to die. He said: "I like it well; I shall die before my heart is soft, or I have said anything unworthy of myself."

Philip, too, no longer cared to live. His tribe was scattered. His wife and children had been taken prisoners and sold as slaves. He was homeless and friendless. Four months after the death of Canonchet he, too, was shot as he was trying to escape from a swamp where he had taken shelter.

The death of these two great sachems ended the war between the white men and the red. But though the war was over, New England was full of grief and mourning. Many of its best and bravest men had been killed. Houses had been burned and towns destroyed. The colonies were in debt for money they had borrowed to pay their troops and to build forts.

It was many a long year before the people ceased to shudder when they remembered the horrors of King Philip's War.

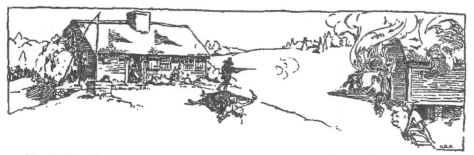

The Indians Resisted, and in the Struggle That Followed One of Them Was Shot

## NOTES

1. Philip's Indian name was Metacom. He was the son of Massasoit, the greatest of the Wampanoag sachems.

2. The Narragansetts and the Wampanoags were the two most powerful tribes of all the New England Indians. At one time the Pequots had ranked with the Wampanoags in fierceness and warlike qualities, but they had been almost destroyed and wiped out by the English some years before.

3. This story has been given by so many authorities that it is here stated as a fact rather than a legend.

4. Accounts differ as to how this wall was made. According to some authors it was built of stones, with a clay wall inside of that, and heavy palisades of logs without. Others say that it consisted of nothing but logs and piles of brushwood; that the Indians would have had to bring the stones and clay from a long distance, and that it is very unlikely that they did this.

5. Mr. W. A. Greene, in his article, "The Great Battle of the Narragansetts," states that only eight of the English were killed in the battle.

Roger Williams Asking the Committee for the Patent

# How, Once Upon A Time, Rhode Island Gained Her Patent

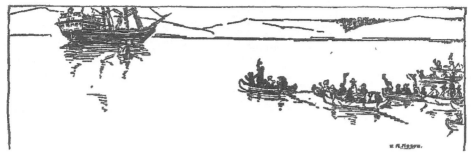

The People of Providence Came Out in Fourteen Canoes

IT WAS late in the spring when Williams and his companions broke ground for their second settlement. Much precious time had already been wasted at Seekonk. It was necessary to get their seed into the ground without delay if they expected it to yield them good crops that year.

The settlers had brought little with them except clothing, tools, and a few cooking utensils. They were obliged not only to plant seeds and build houses for themselves, but they had to make their furniture as well. The building itself was a hard and laborious matter. The houses were made of logs which the settlers had to cut, haul, and raise into place. The chimneys and fireplaces were of unbroken stones fitted together; the cracks between these were filled in with clay. The settlers had no glass for their windows; they had no nails. All the furniture was fastened together with wooden pegs. Rough shutters were closed over the windows when it stormed.

They had brought few provisions with them, and depended largely on their hunting and fishing for food. Everything they had to eat was cooked over open fires, either boiled in pots, or stuck on sharp sticks and roasted before the flames. The Indians who travelled along the Great Bay Path[1] often stopped at the settlement. The most of those who stopped were Narragansetts and seemed very friendly. They watched the work of the white men with some curiosity, but they did not interfere.

No white men had ever ventured so far out into their country before except one, a Mr. William Blackstone. He had built a house not far from where Williams and his companions settled. Blackstone had been a minister in Boston, but suddenly, for what reason no one knew, he had given up the ministry and had come out here into the wilderness to live. He had brought no one with him but his wife. He had built himself a house, laid out fields, and planted an apple orchard. He called his place Study Hill. It was only six miles from Providence, and later on, when the little settlement had grown to be a town, every one in it learned to know Blackstone. He used to ride over from Study Hill on a great white bull that he had trained to carry him as though it were a horse. He would preach to the young men and boys of Providence, and sometimes he would bring them presents of apples — the great juicy "yellow sweetings" that grew in his orchard. These apples were a great curiosity to the boys of that time, for they had never seen an apple until Mr. Blackstone brought the fruit into the town. As soon as Williams had a home for his wife and children they came to join him.[2] Mistress Williams was obliged to leave some of their household goods and possessions behind her in Salem. This distressed Williams greatly. He afterward tried to have the things sent out to Providence, but he was not able to arrange it. The loss of these things was a serious matter to him, for he was very poor, so poor indeed that he was scarcely able to provide the necessary food and clothing for himself and his family. He wrote to a friend that he spent his time both day and night "at the hoe and at the oar for bread," and he spoke with thankfulness of a piece of gold that Governor Winslow put into Mistress Williams's hand one time when he was visiting in Providence. The Indian chiefs Canonicus and Miantonomo had given to Williams about four square miles of land in and about Providence. If he had chosen to sell parts of this to the settlers who came out to join him, he might have made a great deal of money, but this he would not do. Instead, he gave it away, dividing it about equally with the first twelve men who joined him. Each of these men was given a "home lot" the size of his own and six acres of land for fields and pasturing cattle. The "home lots" faced on the "towne street" of the settlement. This "towne street" is now North and South Main streets. It extended as far eastward as the present Hope Street. Williams named his own pasturage "What Cheer" in memory of the greeting called to him from Slate Rock by the friendly Indians. Canonicus was still his close friend, and Williams said that not for thousands of pounds would that great sachem have sold the land to any other Englishman; but to Williams he gave it because of the great love and friendship between them. In a deed, made in March, 1638, Canonicus declared that the land was freely given to Williams "in consideration of the many kindnesses and services he hath continually done for us."

Williams had said he would make of Providence a refuge "for all who were distressed for conscience sake" or who wanted "soul liberty." This promise was so well kept that before long many who wanted religious liberty came out from Plymouth and Massachusetts to join him. It was a great offence to the Puritans that he should give a shelter to all of these and allow them to worship God in any way they pleased. The rulers of Massachusetts and Plymouth would gladly have interfered if they could, but Providence was beyond their boundaries.

Their laws and regulations could not reach out into the wilderness to this new settlement. Some of the settlers who came to Providence for religious freedom felt they ran a great risk in doing so. The risk they feared was not from any Puritan rulers, but from the savages. They could not put the trust in the Indians that Williams seemed to have. They were farther out in the wilderness than any settlers had ever ventured before, and in case of an Indian war Providence would be more open to an attack than almost any other town.

In the summer of 1636 news was brought to Providence that filled these more timid settlers with anxious fears. A war had broken out between the fierce and savage Pequots and the English. The war began with the murder of John Oldham. John Oldham was a Boston man. He and several companions had been in a sloop just off Block Island. The Indians had attacked the sloop, killed John Oldham, and carried his companions off with them into the wilderness. What the savages had done with them, whether they had killed them or were keeping them prisoners, no one knew. Nothing was ever heard of them again.

Many massacres followed this attack upon the sloop. All over the colonies houses were burned, property destroyed, and prisoners tortured. The

English sent out troops to fight the savages, and fortified a number of buildings. Providence took no means to protect itself, and yet it was one of the towns that suffered no harm: not a house was burned nor a settler injured. In October great fears were felt lest the Narragansetts might start out on the warpath, too. They were a very powerful tribe, and if they now took part with the Pequots the war might end in a general massacre of all the English. Governor Vane, of Boston, wrote to Williams and begged him to see the Narragansetts and urge them to keep peace with the English.

It was a wild and stormy day when the Governor's letter was brought to Williams. The wind was howling through the wilderness and whipping the waters of the bay into high waves, but without waiting to make any preparation, hardly even stopping to say good-bye to his wife, Williams launched his canoe and started for the wigwams of the Narragansetts. "The Lord helped me," he wrote, "to put my life in my hand . . . and ship myself alone in a poor canoe, and to cut through a stormy wind with great seas, every minute in hazard of my life, to the sachem's house. Three days and nights my business forced me to lodge and mix with the bloody Pequots' ambassadors, whose hands and arms methought reeked with the blood of my countrymen . . . and from whom I could but nightly look for their bloody knives at my own throat also." In those three days and nights that Williams spent in the Indian wigwams there were long talks and arguments between him and the sachems. Sometimes the Pequots grew so angry that it seemed as though they would fall upon him and murder him. But they feared to do it on account of the Narragansetts, who were still his friends. He afterward wrote of how "God had wondrously preserved me and given me success in my undertaking." For before he returned home he had induced the Narragansetts to break off their treaty with the "bloody Pequots" and to promise that they would keep the peace with the English. It seemed, indeed, a miracle that he was not murdered there among the wigwams. On the fourth day Williams returned home, and a short time afterward several of the sachems went to Boston and there signed a treaty of peace.

It was a brave and daring service that Williams had rendered to the colonies, and he had done it at the risk of his life. For a while afterward there was some talk in Plymouth and Massachusetts of rewarding him or of allowing him at least to return to the colonies; but many of the Puritan leaders were very much opposed to this. They still thought him a dangerous man. Their gratitude to him soon died out and he was still forbidden to set foot inside their boundaries. In 1638 another band of settlers left Massachusetts. They were under the leadership of John Clarke and William Coddington. They also wished to found a settlement where they could have religious freedom. Their plan was to go down to Long Island and settle there. But on their way they stopped at Providence, and Williams urged them to settle on the island of Aquidneck[3] instead of going farther. This they finally decided to do, and a little later, through Williams's advice and help, they bought the whole of the island from the natives. The price paid to Canonicus for the island was "forty fathoms of wampum-peage." Besides

# RHODE ISLAND GAINED HER PATENT

this, the Indians who were living on the island at the time were given ten coats and twenty hoes to make over all their rights in the land to the white men, and the sachem on the island was given five fathoms of wampum-peage.

"Wampum-peage" was the white money of the Indians. They had two kinds, white and black. The white was made of the eyes of perriwinkle shells cut out and smoothed and polished. Six of these were equal to an English penny, and 360 pieces made a fathom. The black peage was made of the black part of round clam shells, and one piece of it was worth two of the white.

Coddington and Clarke and their followers first settled in the northern part of Aquidneck, at Pocasset, now Portsmouth; but the colony grew so fast that before long they separated, and a number of them moved south and settled Newport. These men who settled on the island were, as a rule, very well educated, and were more well-to-do than those who had gone to Providence.

Aquidneck was quite as wild and unbroken as the mainland. There were many deer in the forests there, and these were very valuable to the settlers, both for their skins and as food. The foxes were a great nuisance, and the wolves did so much damage that men were hired by the day to hunt them and kill them. At one time the settlers gathered the Indians together for a great wolf hunt, hoping to clear the island of the beasts. But the work was poorly done. Many wolves escaped. They could still be heard howling in the forests at night and they still visited the settlements and destroyed much live stock.

Four years after the settlement of Aquidneck a man named Samuel Gorton was also banished from Massachusetts and Plymouth and came out to seek a refuge in Providence. He was a very religious man, but of such a curious and difficult nature that he seemed to make trouble wherever he went. After he came to Providence he made so much disturbance that Williams almost decided to leave the town and settle elsewhere.

However, Gorton himself made the move. He went from Providence to Aquidneck to live, but here again he soon found himself in trouble with the settlers. He then bought the lands of Shawomet (afterward Warwick) from the Indians, and he and his followers removed to that place. The price paid for the land was one hundred and forty-four fathoms of wampum-peage.

There were now four settlements in what is now the State of Rhode Island. There was a friendly feeling among these settlements, but each was still entirely separate from the others. Each had its own government and managed its own affairs in its own way. In 1643 the colonies of Massachusetts, Plymouth, Connecticut, and New Haven joined together "for mutual help and succor," and took the name of "The United Colonies of New England." When the news of this union reached Providence it caused a great deal of anxiety. It entirely shut out the smaller settlements, and seemed to mean that in case of any danger the Rhode Island towns would be left to take care of themselves. Yet they were the ones that would need help the most, because they were small and because they could be most easily attacked by either land or sea.

Williams wrote to the Governor of Massachusetts and asked that Providence and the Aquidneck settlements might be allowed to join the league. The answer was eagerly waited for, but when it came it brought only bitter disappointment. The Governor and his assistants refused. The excuse they gave was that the smaller settlements had no patent; neither King nor parliament had given them the right to the lands they were holding. It was now agreed by the three settlements of Providence, Portsmouth, and Newport that they would unite in one colony,[4] and that Williams should go to England and try to get a patent or charter for them. Williams was quite willing to go and at once began to make ready for the voyage. It would have been much easier for him if he had been allowed to set sail from Boston,[5] as that was the nearest port, but he was forbidden to enter that town. Instead he was obliged to journey down to New Amsterdam (now New York City) and set sail from there.

It was a long and tedious journey from America to England in those days. Even the fastest vessels could not cross from one country to another in less than several weeks, and some were months in making the journey. In the months that Williams spent upon the water he began the book he had thought of so long ago — a book about the Indians and their language. Day after day, as the ship rose and fell on the waves, he was busy with his papers, his ink horn, and his quill pen, and by the time he reached England he had made out a rough plan of the volume. He called it "A Key to the Language of America." It not only told about the Indian language, but it related many curious things about their ways and customs and religion as well. The book was finished and printed while Williams was in England and it proved very useful to him. It helped to interest people in Rhode Island and made it easier for him to get the patent.

Parliament, not long before, had appointed a committee to take charge of the affairs of the American colonies. It was from this committee that Williams obtained the patent. It was made out to the "Providence Plantations," for that was the name that was now given to this new colony.

The patent gave to the inhabitants of Providence Plantations the power and the right to govern their affairs in any way they chose to agree upon among themselves — that is, of course, with due regard to right and justice. A letter signed by several members of Parliament was also given to Williams. It was addressed to the Governor of Massachusetts. In it the Governor and assistants were reproved for their bitterness toward Roger Williams, and they were urged to live in greater peace and friendship with their neighbors. With this letter to protect him Williams ventured into Boston harbor and was allowed to land and journey on to Providence Plantations without interference. When he reached Seekonk the people of Providence came out to meet him in fourteen canoes; shouts of welcome filled the air, and he was escorted home in triumph by his grateful people.

But though the four settlements of Rhode Island had now united in one colony, and though they had their patent, there were still troubles ahead of them. It was three years before their government was established, and meanwhile Massachusetts and Plymouth claimed that a part of the Providence Plantations land belonged to them. They said parts of it had been sold to them by the Indians and that they had the first right to it. In 1651 Williams, with John Clarke of Newport, again went to England, to lay the latter before the authorities there and have it settled by them. Once again, as before, all went well with Williams and his mission. Williams was assured that all the land claimed by the Providence Plantations was theirs, and that no other colony had any right to it. With this assurance Williams again returned home, leaving Clarke in England as agent for the colony there. And now Massachusetts and Plymouth no longer dared to lay claim to any part of the new colony. They still refused to admit it to their union, but it stood as their equal, a free and recognized colony with a patent of its own. Soon it was even freer than they, indeed, for in 1663 Charles II gave a charter to the "English Colony of Rhode Island and Providence Plantations" that allowed it such liberty as no other colony had ever received before,[6] a liberty in both civil and religious matters. And this charter has stood, ever since, as one of the most remarkable any king ever gave to any colony.

The First Baptist Meeting House

# NOTES

1. The Great Bay Path followed in general what is now the route of the New York, New Haven, and Hartford Railroad.

2. Roger Williams's son, Providence, born in the autumn of 1638, is said to have been the first male child born in Rhode Island.

3. The name of the Island of Aquidneck was changed to the Isle of Rhodes, or Rhode Island, in 1644.

4. Warwick was not joined to the Providence Plantations until 1649.

5. Besides the inconvenience, Williams's exclusion from Boston was a great loss to him from a money standpoint. He wrote to his friend Major Mason that his being "debarred from Boston, the chief mart and port of New England," had been a cause of great loss to him in the way of trade. "God knows," he wrote, "that many thousand pounds cannot repay the losses I have sustained."

6. The Rhode Island Charter is one of the most liberal charters ever granted by England to a colony. Not only did it give to the people of Rhode Island the right (so long as they made no laws contrary to the laws of England) to govern themselves; but it also gave to the inhabitants complete religious liberty. No person in the colony was to be "molested, punished, disquieted, or called in question for any difference in opinion in matters of religion." Even the people of England at that time had less religious liberty than this charter gave to the people of Rhode Island.

"Stand Off, You Can't Come on Board!"

# How, Once Upon A Time, The People Of Rhode Island Destroyed The "Gaspee"

R—R—Rum—Chum—Dum!

IT WAS March of the year 1772 when the armed British schooner *Gaspee* sailed into Narragansett Bay. Her sails were set wide to the light wind, and the British colors fluttered at her masthead.

Many angry and unfriendly eyes watched her coming. Not that the people of Rhode Island were unfriendly to all, or even many, of the British armed vessels. The most of them would have been welcome in the bay. But the *Gaspee* was different from these. She had been sent over from England for a certain purpose, and a purpose that ill-pleased the merchants and shipowners of Rhode Island.

For over a hundred years the British Parliament had been making laws to regulate the American trade and to tell the traders what they might or might not do; but until the year 1763 England had made almost no effort to have these laws obeyed. The colonists traded as they pleased, and managed their own affairs with little interference from the mother country.

But from the year 1763 England began to try to

enforce the laws that had been so long neglected, and this caused a great deal of trouble and disturbance in America. The colonists had been left free so long that now they were little disposed to submit to any regulations made by the mother country.

One law that the colonists most resented was that they must pay a tax, or duty, to England on a great many articles they used and that were brought in from other countries, such articles as sugar, tea, rum, molasses, and so on.

There were officers whose duty it was to collect the taxes on these things. They were called customs officers.

In past years the customs officers had been very careless about their duties. Many things that should have been taxed were brought into the colonies without anything being paid on them. This was of course smuggling, but to most of the colonists it did not seem wrong; as the laws about taxation seemed unjust they saw no harm in breaking them. Some, indeed, felt it was a brave and patriotic thing to do.

But now England ordered the customs officers to be very strict about collecting the taxes. The colonial governors were ordered to help the officers in every way they could, and several British armed vessels were sent over and stationed along the coasts to see that no smuggling was carried on. The *Gaspee* was one of these.

In 1763 Rhode Island owned more vessels in proportion to her size and population than any other colony.[1] Many of them were small, of course, and sailed only up and down the bay or to the nearby colonies. But there were many larger ships, owned

## THE PEOPLE DESTROYED THE "GASPEE"

by people in Providence or Newport or Bristol, and these vessels sailed away on longer journeys. Often they were gone for months, or even years. They visited strange countries, and when they returned they brought rich cargoes of sugar, molasses, spices, silks, and other valuable things. It seemed both unjust and unreasonable to the Rhode Island men that they should be expected to pay a tax to England on things they had bought with their own money and were bringing home in their own vessels to their own home ports.

In 1764 the British schooner *St. John* had sailed into Narragansett Bay and had made herself very troublesome to the traders by stopping their boats, examining their cargoes, and fining them if duties had not been paid. This was so troublesome, indeed, that before long the people of Newport began to lay plans to destroy her. No doubt they would have done so, too, if a second English ship, the *Squirrel*, had not arrived. Two armed vessels, each ready to defend the other, were more than even the brave men of Newport dared to attack. So no attempt to harm them was made. But that same year, when the British frigate *Maidstone* anchored in the bay, the people of Newport seized her long-boats and carried them up to the Common in front of the courthouse and there burned them, shouting and cheering as the flames blazed up from the hated English boats.

In 1769 the armed sloop *Liberty*, commanded by Captain Reid, began to cruise about our waters, stopping boats and examining their cargoes. Among the boats that were overhauled was a brig commanded by Captain Packwood. Captain Reid examined the brig's cargo, and soon found that all the duties had been paid. But for some reason some of Captain Packwood's clothes were carried on board the *Liberty* and were not returned to him.

A little later Captain Packwood had himself rowed over to the *Liberty* and went on board to get his clothes himself; but the head officer refused to give them to him, and so ill-used him that he was glad to escape even without his clothes, and get back to his brig with a whole skin. Several muskets were fired after him as he went, and it was only good luck that he and his sailors were not wounded by the shots.

Captain Reid was not on board the *Liberty* at the time. He had gone ashore for the day. That evening when he came down to the water-side to return to his ship he was stopped by a great crowd of angry Newport people. They warned him that they intended to destroy the *Liberty*, and that he had better send for all his men to come ashore.

Captain Reid looked from one to another of the angry faces around him. He saw the men meant what they said, and he was wise enough to take their advice. He ordered all his own men to leave the ship, and very soon after they left her she was boarded by the Newport men and brought up to the Long Wharf. There her masts were cut away, and she was sunk; but her boats were carried up to the Common and burned, as those of the *Maidstone* had been burned five years before.

But hated as all the English vessels had been, none was as bitterly hated as the *Gaspee* in 1772. Her commander, Lieutenant Duddingston, was an insolent, overbearing man. He seemed to take pride

## THE PEOPLE DESTROYED THE "GASPEE"

in stopping the traffic of the bay. Even the little market-boats were stopped and searched as though he expected to find sugar or rum or molasses hidden under the vegetables. The farmers complained that much of their produce was being ruined or destroyed by him. If vessels that were hailed did not stop immediately a shot was fired across their bows as a warning of what they might expect if they did not wait to be searched. Duddingston seemed to take particular pleasure in terrorizing the people in the smaller boats. People were almost afraid to cross the water from one town to another even on visits.

Sometimes after a vessel had been searched the lieutenant would declare that the proper duties had not been paid on its cargo. If the owner complained and insisted that the duties had been paid, the articles were perhaps taken from him and sent on to Boston for the question to be decided there.[2] This was very inconvenient for the owners, and often caused them a heavy loss. Moreover, it was contrary to an act of Parliament which provided that all such cases must be tried in the same colony in which the articles had been seized.

The *Gaspee* had not been in our waters long before complaints about her began to come to the ears of the Governor of Rhode Island. The Governor wrote to Duddingston remonstrating with him for the way the traffic was being interrupted, but he received a most insolent answer. A second letter to the lieutenant went unanswered, but Admiral Montague, the commander of the British fleet, wrote to the Governor from Boston ordering him not to interfere with Duddingston in any way. The admiral's letter was even more insolent in tone than his lieutenant's had been.

But while these letters were being exchanged between the Governor and the British commanders, the Rhode Island people were remembering Captain Reid and longing to serve the *Gaspee* as the *Liberty* had once been served.

It was on June 9th that Captain Thomas Lindsay set sail from the harbor of Newport, on his way to Providence. He knew the *Gaspee* would probably see him and that her men would try to stop him and search his cargo, but he made up his mind not to allow this if he could help it. It was with all his sails spread that he swept out of the harbor and started on his way.

As he expected, he had not gone far before he was sighted by the *Gaspee*. A shot was fired across his bows as a warning for him to stop, but without paying any attention to this the gallant captain kept on his way.

The *Gaspee* now started in pursuit of the packet-boat, but "a stern chase is a long chase," and the packet was hard to overtake.

About seven miles below Providence the shore runs out in a long spit of land called Namquit Point. The packet swept around this point, leaning far over to the brisk wind. Hoping to overtake her, the *Gaspee* tried to cut across a shallow place, but the water was even shallower than her commander had thought, and to the rage of the lieutenant she ran aground. Then there was a great running and shouting on board of her; orders were given and followed out in haste, but they were of no use. The *Gaspee* lay there in the hot summer sunlight careening

## THE PEOPLE DESTROYED THE "GASPEE"

over more and more as the hours passed by and the water sank away from her, for the tide was on the ebb. Before long it was clear that not only had she missed her chance of catching the packet, but that she would have to stay where she was until high tide, and that would not be until three o'clock the next morning.

Meantime Captain Lindsay sailed quietly on to Providence, reaching there some time in the late afternoon.

No sooner had he landed than he went straight to the house of Mr. John Brown, who was a great friend of his. Here he told his story of how the English schooner had tried to overtake and stop him, how it had run aground, and how even now it was lying there off Namquit Point and would not be able to float again until the next morning.

It did not take the friends long to decide that now was the chance to rid themselves of the hated schooner forever. Nor did they doubt that there were plenty of men in Providence who would be eager to join them in the bold adventure of destroying it.

It was about two hours after sunset that same evening when the long roll of a drum suddenly sounded at the upper end of Main Street in Providence, that long "towne street" that Roger Williams had laid out so many years before. R-r-rum-dum-dum! R-r-r-rum-dum-dum! Many stopped to listen to the call of the drum. Then it was still and a man was heard calling out in a loud voice:

"The *Gaspee* has run aground on Namquit Point, and cannot float before three o'clock tomorrow morning! Those persons who feel disposed to go and destroy that troublesome vessel are invited to repair to Mr. James Sabin's house this evening!"

Then again sounded the long roll of the drum. On down the street came the drummer; a pause, and again the message was shouted through the twilight.

Of those who heard there were many who were eager to answer to the call. Before nine o'clock that evening a company of men had gathered in the long, low southeast room of Mr. Sabin's house.

This house of Mr. Sabin's was an inn[3] at the corner of what are now South Main and Planet streets, and directly across from Fenner's wharf.

The people who gathered there were armed, some with guns, some with pistols. Those who had no arms themselves had borrowed from their neighbors. They had very few bullets, however, so a fire was lighted in the great fireplace, and lead was hurriedly melted and poured into bullet moulds.

Eight of the largest long-boats in the town had been brought up to Fenner's wharf and fastened there. The rowlocks and oars were now carefully muffled so that they could be used without making any noise. By ten o'clock everything was ready, the men entered the boats, and the expedition set out. Captain Whipple was put in command.

On their way down the river the boats were stopped at Captain Cook's wharf and some of the men got for themselves paving-stones and staves. Then on they went again through the darkness, down past Fox Point, and around Field's Point, and so on toward where the *Gaspee* lay.

So silent were they that they had come close to

the schooner before the watch discovered their approach. Then his cry rang out, "Who comes there?"

No answer was made from the boats. Still in silence they glided on toward the *Gaspee*.

Lieutenant Duddingston had heard his sentinel's call and had hurried on deck, and now he himself hailed them, his voice ringing out through the darkness: "Who comes there?"

Captain Whipple answered: "I want to come on board."

"Stand off! You can't come on board!" called the lieutenant.

With a string of oaths Captain Whipple roared out: "I am the sheriff of the county of Kent; I am come for the commander of this vessel, and have him I will, dead or alive. Men, spring to your oars!"

Almost at the same moment Joseph Bucklin, one of the men in the boats, said to a companion, "Eph, reach me your gun. I can kill that fellow." He meant Lieutenant Duddingston. The gun was handed to him and a shot rang out.

Lieutenant Duddingston gave a groan and sank down on the companion-way. "I'm done for!" he exclaimed. Bucklin had shot him through the groin.

Other shots followed, the men on the *Gaspee* firing rather wildly through the darkness, but no one else was wounded except a British sailor, who was shot in the head by some one in the long-boat. A few minutes later the Providence men had boarded the schooner, and the English seamen had surrendered to them without a blow.

Lieutenant Duddingston was helped down to the cabin, and Captain Whipple immediately sent Dr. John Mawney down to dress his wounds. As soon as this was done, and the lieutenant had been made as comfortable as possible, he and his men were hurried down into the boats and rowed over to the Warwick side, and were put ashore there at the Still-house wharf.

The Providence men returned to the *Gaspee* and set her on fire, and then drew off to a safe distance. Presently smoke began to rise from the schooner. It grew in volume, sweeping out like a black cloud and darkening the waters. Tongues of flame licked across the deck and up into the rigging.

Silently the Providence men watched, resting on their oars. Suddenly their boat was shaken by the dull roar of an explosion. A mass of burning wood and rigging was shot high above the schooner and fell back into the water with a great splash. Bits of burning wood were thrown through the air even as far as where the long-boats lay.

The powder in the *Gaspee* had exploded, blowing her to bits. Nothing was now left but the floating wreckage and a part of the hull. The night's work was finished and the *Gaspee* was destroyed.

Still very quietly the long-boats were rowed back to town. The men who were in them separated and returned each to his own home.

The strange thing is that the authorities who wished to punish these men for burning the schooner never were able to find out who they were. Almost every one in the town must have known, but no one would tell.

Governor Wanton offered a reward of $500 for any

information as to who they were. The King of England offered $5,000 reward for the leader of the expedition and $2,500 for the arrest of any of the men who had been with him, but no one could be bribed or frightened into betraying the patriots who had delivered their colony from the hated *Gaspee*.

The Sabin House in 1880

## NOTES

1. In 1763 the citizens of Rhode Island owned more than 500 vessels, great and small, and more than 2,200 seamen were engaged in sailing them.

2. Among the articles thus seized and sent to Boston were twelve hogsheads of rum belonging to Nathanael Greene, Jr., he who was afterward one of our great generals in the Revolutionary War.

3. The house is described as "a house of board and entertainment for gentlemen."

Miss Peggy Champlin's Cheeks Grew Pinker and Pinker

# How, Once Upon A Time, Newport Learned About War

*It Became a Fashion with the French Officers to Write Upon the Window Panes*

BEFORE the time of the Revolution Newport was one of the gayest and richest of all the New England towns. It was one of the most beautiful as well. It lay upon a hill that slopes gently down to the waters of a harbor, a harbor so wide and deep that all the fleets of the country could anchor there and still leave room for more.

The fineness of the harbor led many shipowners to settle in Newport in the early days. In a few years its shipping interests became more important than those of any other town in the colonies except Boston and New York.

Other people besides shipowners were led to settle at Newport by one reason or another. Many Jews and Quakers[1] came because of the religious freedom they found there; others came because of the mild and delightful climate,[2] and still others for the sake of the gay life of the town, or for its science and learning.

Many of the Newport merchants became very wealthy. They built handsome houses[3] and filled them with fine furniture. Gay lawns laid out with terraces and flower-beds stretched down to the shining water. Often the merchants had slaves to wait on them and take care of their children, for Rhode Island was a slave-trading colony. In colonial times it carried on a larger slave-trade for its size than any other colony.[4]

Many fine feasts and gay balls were given by the Newport people of those days, and there was much visiting back and forth between them and the Narragansett people, on the other side of the bay, for the fashionable folk of Narragansett were as gay as those of Newport, and just as fond of ease and luxury and good eating.

The Quakers of the town could not take part in the dances and music and gay feasts; they could not wear ribbons and laces and bright-colored silks like the fashionable folk. Their religion forbade all those things. Their clothes must be plain in cut and color. They had to use plain language and say "thee" and "thou" instead of "you". But their Quaker suits and dresses were generally made of the very best materials[5] (for that was allowed), and there were no houses where brighter silver or finer linen could be found than in some of the Quaker homes, and no place where the people had better things to eat and drink, either.

And then there were simpler merry-makings than balls and feasts, in which even the young Quakers and Quakeresses could join. There were corn huskings and sewing and spinning bees. An old newspaper printed in 1767 tells how "thirty-seven young ladies of the town" went one afternoon to spin yarn for Mrs. Stiles, a clergyman's wife. They sent their wheels and carried flax enough for a moderate day's spinning. They worked so busily and well that by sunset they were able to hand over to Mrs. Stiles "a present of one hundred skeins of yarn, fine enough for shirts for the best gentlemen in America."

No doubt those young ladies of long ago had a merry time as they sat there, spinning and gossiping and laughing through the long afternoon, and perhaps having a cup of tea with Mrs. Stiles before they went home again.

The Newport newspaper of those days was the *Mercury*. The press on which it was printed was brought to Newport in 1730 by James Franklin,[6] and later on it passed into the hands of Mr. Solomon Southwick, the publisher of the *Mercury*. The press was worked by hand and the type was often rough and blurred. The newspaper itself was no larger than an ordinary sheet of writing-paper, but it was thought a very good paper in those days; it was read as eagerly by people then as our large sheets are read by the people nowadays.

There was a great deal of learning in Newport: the Redwood Library[7] held a very fine collection of books, finer indeed than was to be found in any other town in the colonies except Cambridge.

But suddenly into all this pleasant, easy life of Newport there came terror and confusion and poverty.

Late in the summer of 1775 several British vessels sailed into the harbor and anchored there. In October they were joined by four more war vessels, and their commander, Captain Wallace, sent a demand that the country people around Newport should supply him with a large amount of provisions and livestock. Some they could give him, but not as much as he asked for.

The people of the town became very much alarmed. They were afraid his vessels might fire on the town and burn and destroy it, as they had already destroyed the town of Falmouth in Maine.

Furniture, goods, and chattels were packed, and the people fled back into the country where they would be out of range of the cannon. Some of them buried silver and other valuables in their cellars before leaving. Mr. Southwick made a hole in the yard of an old building on Broad Street[8] and buried his press there, so that it might not fall into the hands of the British.

As the panic grew the streets became almost blocked by the people hurrying to leave. Some were in carriages, some in carts, and some on foot. Frightened fathers and mothers pushed their way through the crowd carrying bundles and dragging crying children by the hand. People were filled with only one thought, that of escaping from the town.

When the news of this panic came to the ears of Wallace he was very much disturbed. He had not meant to frighten the people into leaving Newport. The things they were carrying away with them might be very useful to him later on, if he quartered his men in the town.

In order to give the people confidence he decided to sail away for a time, and leave Newport to settle down in peace.

So one day those who were watching saw that the dreaded British war vessels were hauling up their anchors, sails were being set, and, presently, one after another the great ships got under way, and slowly sailed out of the harbor.

The greatest relief was felt in Newport over their going. Many people returned to their homes. Furniture was unpacked and the business of life was taken up again. But the relief did not last long. Shortly the fleet was back in the harbor, and this time the British landed and took possession of the town.[9]

The people were in despair. They dared not leave Newport now, for if they did they would not be allowed to carry any of their things with them. Everything they had would be kept by the British or destroyed. The British showed no respect for anything. A number of buildings that were of no use to them they burned. Churches were used for stables. The Colony House was turned into a hospital. All trading between Newport and the other colonies was stopped. The press that Mr. Southwick had buried[10] was found by the British and cleaned and set up, and they used it to print a paper of their own in favor of the King. Many of the other things that had been hidden were found by them and confiscated.

Before the winter was over the suffering among the inhabitants was very great. Many people who had been wealthy were now so poor that they had not even enough to eat. Food was scarce and high. Corn cost four dollars a bushel, and potatoes two dollars. Wood was worth twenty dollars a cord. Several old houses were torn down and used for fuel. A ship was hauled up on the shore and broken to pieces, and people eagerly gathered up the planks and carried them home to burn. Help was sent the sufferers from the other colonies — food, clothing, wood, and money — but not enough came to meet the bitter need of the people.

For four years the British held possession of the town, and for four years the suffering and poverty grew greater and greater.

Then in 1779 it began to be whispered about that the British were going to leave Newport. The people hardly dared to believe this: it seemed too good to be true. But in October ships and transports began to gather in the harbor. Then came an order that on a certain day all the inhabitants of the town must keep within doors upon pain of death; the British were going to embark for New York.

All the day of the embarkation the inhabitants were shut in their houses, but they could hear from without in the streets shouts and orders, and the tramp of marching feet. There were other sounds, too; sounds of chopping and tearing, the crash of falling timber, and the clang of metal. Those who looked from the windows could see columns of smoke rising from different parts of the town. Later on the British began to form in troops and march down toward the harbor, and by night they had all gone. The streets lay silent and deserted. At last the inhabitants could leave their houses. But those who ventured out found a ruined Newport.[11] Before leaving, the British had destroyed everything they could. They had filled up the wells; they had cut down almost all the trees; the beautiful lawns and orchards were laid waste. The lighthouse at Beaver Tail had been burned; four hundred and eighty buildings were destroyed; the wharves had been broken up and the British had carried off with them the town records[12] that had been kept since the earliest settlement of the town, and much valuable machinery, and all the church bells but one. That one they left because it had been a present to the church from Queen Anne.

It seemed impossible that Newport could ever again become a prosperous, thriving town; the ruin had been too great.

It was in the next summer, that of 1780, that news was brought to Newport that another fleet was coming to anchor in her harbor. But this news was received with joy, for the vessels that were coming were from France, and the French were our good friends and allies, and were coming to help us in our war with England.

Poor as Newport now was, it made ready to show the Frenchmen that its people were as gay and hospitable as ever, in spite of their poverty. When the fleet arrived a warm welcome was given to the visitors. The best of all the city had left was offered to them, and a number of balls and dinners were given.

The French returned these entertainments with other gayeties that they tried to make as brilliant as possible. They were delighted with the people of Newport. They admired their freshness and simplicity and refinement. They seemed particularly charmed with the quiet, simple life of the Quakers.

It became a fashion with the French officers to write upon the window panes, with their diamond rings, the names of the young ladies they considered most beautiful or charming, and the name of many a Newport belle was to be seen on the panes of the Newport houses. Unluckily almost all those panes of glass have been broken and the names have disappeared with them, or are left only in old letters and books. The Count de Rochambeau, who had come over with the fleet, had his headquarters at the Vernon House, at the corner of Clarke and Mary streets, and it was in this house that Washington was entertained when he came to Newport in March, 1781.

This visit of Washington's was felt to be a great event for the town. Every possible preparation was made to do him honor, not only by the people of Newport but by their French visitors as well.

When the day came that had been set for his arrival the French admiral's own barge was sent over to the Conanicut side to meet him, and as it brought him across the harbor the cannon of the French fleet fired a salute to him. Again and again they thundered out their salute to the Commander-in-chief of the American army.

A great crowd had gathered at Ferry Dock to see Washington land. They cheered and waved their hats as he stepped out of the barge, and all the bells in the town began to ring.

The French troops were lined up three deep on each side of the street all the way from the dock to the Vernon House. As Washington passed between them the sound of cheering on either side swept on with him like a great wave, and above all the noise the bells kept up their clanging.

The people of Newport were anxious to have Washington see their town, and a torchlight procession had been arranged for that evening to escort him through the streets. Many of the people who wished to take part in this procession were so poor that they could not afford to buy a torch to carry.

The Town Council, therefore, ordered a great quantity of candles to be bought and given to those who could not buy for themselves.

Thirty boys headed the procession, carrying candles fixed on the ends of sticks, then came Washington, with Rochambeau and an escort of citizens and French officers.

Very fortunately the night was clear and still. There was not a breath of air to blow the lights of the torches. Washington could be plainly seen by the throngs along the streets, and those who crowded the windows of the houses. He was a very tall man, taller by half a head than any of his escort, and he had a serene and noble face. When they returned to the Vernon House Washington stopped on the top step, and, turning, thanked the boys who had carried the candles.

One little lad, too young to march with the others, had heard a great deal about Washington, and what a great thing it was to see him. He thought Washington must be some very strange and wonderful being, and begged his father to lift him up so he could look. The father raised the little fellow to his shoulder and pointed out the general to him. The child stared and stared with disappointed eyes. Then he cried, "Why, father, Washington is nothing but a man!" In his disappointment his little voice rose so high and clear through the still night that Washington heard him. He smiled. "Yes, my lad," he answered back, "*and nothing but a man.*"

The day after his arrival was spent by Washington and Rochambeau in talking over the state of the country and planning the spring and summer campaigns. But at four o'clock all business was put aside and they sat down to a fine dinner. The room where they ate was the large, square dining-room of the Vernon House, facing on Mary Street. It had been handsomely decorated with French flags, crossed swords, and a quantity of silver that the French had brought with them.

In the evening a ball was given for Washington by the officers at Mrs. Cowley's Assembly Rooms on Church Street, three doors from Thames Street. These rooms had also been handsomely decorated by the officers and the ladies.

Balls began earlier in those days than now, and very soon after dinner the guests began to arrive on foot, or in their heavy, old-time coaches. The ladies wore flowered silks, gay satins and laces, and the gentlemen were just as fine in their embroidered waistcoats, long coats, satin breeches, and glittering buckles.

Washington was to open the ball, and he chose for his partner Miss Peggy Champlin. Miss Champlin was perhaps not the most beautiful of the young ladies at the ball, but she had a grace and sweetness that charmed every one who saw her.

As Washington took her hand to lead her out, whispers and glances passed between the French officers. Rochambeau and his suite crossed to where the musicians were sitting, took their place, and began themselves to play for the dance. As a compliment to Washington the one chosen was "The Successful Campaign." The figures in it were very much like the figures in the Virginia Reel, but it was danced in a slower and more dignified manner.

Miss Peggy Champlin's cheeks grew pinker and pinker as she walked through the figures of the dance, and curtsied and gave her hand to her tall partner. To be dancing with the great Washington, the Commander-in-chief of the whole American army, seemed almost more honor than she could bear.

The ball was the last of the entertainments given in honor of Washington. The next day he left Newport and soon was back in camp, cheering up his soldiers, planning battles, and winning victory and freedom for his country.

But many a long year afterward the people of Newport loved to remember and talk about the ball where Washington danced "The Successful Campaign" with their Newport belle, pretty Peggy Champlin.

Those Who Looked from the Windows Could See Columns of Smoke Rising from Different Parts of the Town

# NOTES

1. The Society of Friends, or Quakers as they were commonly called, was established in Rhode Island in very early times. The first record of their monthly meeting is dated 1676.

2. Many attribute the mildness of Newport to the course of the Gulf stream, which, by a sudden curve, almost washes the shores of the island.

3. Colonel Godfrey Malbone's house, just outside of Newport, was said to be the finest house in all the colonies.

4. Rhode Island's large slave-trade is, perhaps, largely attributable to the influence of the many West Indians who came to spend the summer at Newport. The slaves of Rhode Island were, however, emancipated in 1784, and the introduction of slaves into the state, on any pretext whatever, was forbidden.

5. The dress of a young Quakeress of 1780 is thus described by one of the French officers: "A kind of English dress, fitting the figure closely, and was white as milk; a muslin apron of the same color, and a large handkerchief gathered close around the neck." On her head she wore "a simple little cap of *baptiste*, with round plaits."

6. A brother of Benjamin Franklin.

7. Named after Abraham Redwood, one of the leading citizens of Newport. He gave £500 for the purchase of standard books in London, and recommended building a library for them, and also for such other books as might be purchased for Newport. Mr. Redwood was a Quaker.

8. This building was known as the Kilburn House.

9. The troops quartered on the town numbered 8,000 English and Hessians.

10. The press was set up in the Vaughan House, which stood at the corner of Parade and Thames streets.

11. "Newport never recovered from the cruel blow. More than half the population had forsaken the island, and the commerce that once filled its crowded wharves was either annihilated or had sought less hazardous resorts, never to return. The Jews, whose enterprise had done so much for their adopted state, had all left the town."— (Arnold's "History of the State of Rhode Island.")

At the time the British left the town the number of inhabitants was reduced from 12,000 to 4,000.

12. "The vessel containing these precious papers was sunk at Hurl Gate. Three years afterward the half-obliterated fragments were returned to the town, and a copy was made of such portions as were still legible." (Arnold's "History of the State of Rhode Island.") Other of the records have since been restored and bound.

She Was the "Glasgow"

# How, Once Upon A Time, A Rhode Island Man Became The First Admiral Of The American Navy

Hopkins Departing for the Alfred

UP TO the year 1775 the American colonies had no navy. When the troubles with England began English ships could sail our waters and enter our harbors unhindered, for we had no vessels able to defend us.

Rhode Island was the first of all the colonies to see that she needed armed vessels to protect her, and her assembly ordered two frigates to be fitted out for this purpose.

Later on it was the Rhode Island delegates who urged on Congress the need of having a navy as well as an army. Other delegates followed the lead of those from Rhode Island in urging it, and in October of 1775 Congress ordered two "swift-sailing vessels" to be fitted out as warships. In December it ordered thirteen more warships to be built.

A Marine Committee was appointed to have charge of all naval matters. It would also be necessary to appoint an admiral to command the fleet, and the choice of a man for this position was a very important matter. We were on the brink of a war with a great and powerful nation. There would be battles on the sea as well as by land. The commander of the navy would be second in importance only to the commander of the army, and the best man must be chosen for the position.

Captain Esek Hopkins[1] was a Rhode Island man. Like many of the men of his colony, he had been used to the sea all his life. He had made many voyages, he had captured several prizes, and he was part owner of more than one good sailing vessel. The farm where he and his wife[2] and family lived was just outside of Providence. Even though he had been away from home so much, his neighbors had learned to look to him as a man of good sense and judgment.

At the time the war with England broke out Captain Hopkins was almost sixty years old, but he was still strong and energetic and daring. He was a handsome man, with well-shaped features, large, flashing dark eyes, and a determined look.

In the summer of 1775 a great deal of fear was felt in Providence lest the British fleet should enter the harbor. Captain Hopkins was put in charge of its defences. He arranged a floating battery, fire-ships, and a boom and chain that could be stretched across the mouth of the harbor if necessary. These protections were so strong that no British vessel dared to try to enter there.

Captain Hopkins was also put in command of the colonial forces in Rhode Island. When the British fleet was anchored at Newport and threatening the town, Hopkins marched to its relief with his troops, and did much to protect it from the enemy. He served his colony well in many other ways besides.

This was the man who was chosen by unanimous vote of Congress to be the head of the navy. His title was to be, not only Admiral and Commodore, but Commander-in-chief of the Navy, just as Washington's title was Commander-in-chief of the Army.

As soon as Commodore Hopkins heard of his appointment he gave up his command of the Rhode Island forces, enlisted one hundred Rhode Island men to serve on his vessels, and set sail for Philadelphia. Here he was very busy inspecting his vessels and planning out a cruise that was to begin early in January.

He was not satisfied with the size of his squadron, however. He felt he needed more vessels for what he had to do. With the consent of Congress he ordered eight merchantmen to be fitted out as additional warships.

Lord Dunmore, with a squadron of British vessels, had been raiding the towns along the southern coast and capturing arms, ammunition, and other supplies. The first order that Congress gave the Commodore was to sail down to the relief of these southern colonies.

The 9th of January, 1775, was the day chosen for the fleet to set sail. The weather that winter was very cold and the river was filled with floating blocks of ice. The admiral's flagship, the *Alfred*, was anchored out almost opposite the foot of Walnut Street, and the other vessels[3] lay as near it and each other as was safe. No mast in all the little fleet as yet showed either flag or pennant. Not until the Commodore took command would they raise their colors.

Very early in the morning of the 9th crowds began to gather down by the river. They had come to see the Commodore embark. A barge lay waiting for him at the Walnut Street wharf.

A little before nine o'clock those who had managed to find a place close to the barge heard the crowds farther up the street cheering. The sound came nearer and nearer. Then a way opened through the throng, and the Commodore appeared with his escort, and stepped into the barge. His bold and handsome face was somewhat reddened by the cold wind. For the sake of warmth he wore a long cloak over his uniform. His hat was three-cornered, and his hair unpowdered.

As he entered the barge a roar of artillery sounded across the water. It was a salute to the Commander of the Navy.

The oarsmen had some trouble in making their way through the floating cakes of ice, but they reached the *Alfred* without any accident, and the Commodore mounted to her deck.

As he boarded her, her Captain, Saltonstall, gave the signal and Lieutenant John Paul Jones ran up the first flag of our American Navy to the masthead. The flag was of yellow silk. The design upon it was a pine tree and a rattlesnake. Above this design were the words, "*An Appeal to God*"; below, the threatening warning, "*Don't tread on me.*"

When those on shore saw the fluttering bit of silk slide up to the masthead a great shout burst from them. Hats were waved or thrown up in the air. Everywhere there was the greatest enthusiasm.

And now all was stir and bustle aboard the fleet. Anchors were hauled in, sails set, the great ships leaned to the chill wind, and slowly they began to move off on their way to the Delaware Capes and the open ocean.

But the river was so blocked with ice that it was

a full month before the squadron sailed out between the Capes. The weather turned stormy, with sleet and hail that coated masts and decks and rigging with ice. Before they had been out long many of the men fell ill, and were no longer able to do their share of the work. Two of the vessels became separated from the fleet and did not rejoin it until some time later.[4]

Beaten and battered by storms, the fleet reached the southern coast at last. They found that the British squadron had taken shelter in a harbor there, where they were protected by the guns on shore. Their position was a very strong one — so strong, in fact, that Commodore Hopkins dared not attack them. He would run too great a risk of having his fleet crippled, while he himself would be able to do but little damage to the enemy. Moreover, few of his men were in a condition to fight. Many of them were so ill they were scarcely able to crawl about the decks.

After carefully considering all this Commodore Hopkins decided to sail down toward the Bahama Islands. He had learned that the English had stored there, at the town of New Providence, a large supply of arms and ammunition. These arms and ammunition would be of the greatest use to the government at home if he could capture them.

It was early in March when the fleet reached the islands and sailed into the harbor of New Providence.

The town had, at that time, two forts overlooking the harbor. The arms and supplies were stored in the larger one of these. When the American fleet appeared many of the inhabitants of the town fled from their houses and took refuge in this fort.

Commodore Hopkins landed two hundred marines and fifty sailors, and marched first upon the smaller fort. He hoped to take it without much difficulty. As a matter of fact, no attempt at defence was made; the gates of the fort were opened to the Americans, and its keys and everything in it were handed over to them.

The Commodore now sent out a proclamation saying he had only come to New Providence for the arms and ammunition, and if these were made over to him all private property would be left untouched, and no harm would come to any of the inhabitants of the town.

As soon as those who had taken shelter in the fort heard this proclamation they quietly went back to their own homes. Not enough men stayed in the fort even to fire the guns, and the Governor could not do otherwise than open the gates to the Americans and let them take what they would. Not a shot was fired on either side, not a man was wounded.

Commodore Hopkins found an even larger supply of arms and ammunition than he had hoped. There were eighty-eight cannon, fifteen mortars, round shot and powder, and a large store of shells. This was indeed a valuable lot to have captured, and without bloodshed.

The marines and sailors at once set to work carrying the booty down to the seashore and loading it on the vessels. It was a heavy cargo for the little fleet — so heavy, indeed, that they could not carry it all. The Commodore was obliged to borrow a sloop to help. This sloop he promised to return as soon as he landed its cargo at home.

When all was ready the fleet began to make its way

slowly northward. The load it carried was too heavy for fast sailing. The vessels stayed together as much as possible, and a careful lookout was kept for any of the enemy's craft.

Overloaded as the vessels were, they would have been in a bad position if they had fallen in with the enemy's fleet. Two British vessels they did meet on the way north. One was the schooner *Hawk*, and the other the brig *Bolton*. They were both small craft, however, and in spite of the cargo our vessels were carrying they managed to capture both of them, and took them on with them as prizes.

By the night of April 6th the fleet had reached Long Island Sound. One of the smaller vessels was in the lead; the *Cabot* followed, and the others were not far behind.

Just outside the Sound the lights of an unknown vessel were seen. The small craft that was in the lead hailed her. The answer from the stranger was a broadside that showed she carried a number of heavy guns. She showed too much strength indeed for the smaller vessel to dare to engage with her. It drew off and made haste to escape through the darkness.

Later on three other vessels of the fleet, the *Cabot*, the *Alfred*, and the *Andrea Doria*, came up, and each in turn fired on the stranger. Their shots were returned, and for three hours a brisk fight was kept up. The American vessels suffered considerable damage. Ten men were killed and many more were severely injured.[5] The vessels were so over-weighted with their cargoes that they were not able to engage as closely as they might otherwise have done, and each of the three was forced, in turn, to withdraw from the fight.

Dawn was now breaking across the water. In the growing light the strange vessel loomed up huge and dark. The smoke of her broadside still curled across the water and mingled with the morning mist. She was the *Glasgow*, a British war vessel of twenty-four guns. She, too, had suffered in the engagements. Some of her masts were splintered, and part of her rigging torn away.

While it was still scarcely light the *Columbus*, with Captain Whipple in command, came bearing down on her.

The *Glasgow* was too much damaged to meet this new attack. She took to flight, making off in the direction of Newport. The *Columbus* followed in hot pursuit of her.

Commodore Hopkins saw with anxiety the direction that the chase was taking. The British squadron lay in Newport Harbor, and he feared it might be drawn out and attack him. He signaled Captain Whipple to give up the chase. This the gallant Captain was very loth to do, but he dared not disobey. The *Columbus* returned to its place in the fleet, and the whole squadron sailed on and reached New London without further adventure.

When the news became known through the colonies that the Admiral had returned from this first cruise with valuable prizes, and without having lost a single man, there was great rejoicing. Praises were heaped on the Commander-in-chief. Congress itself passed a resolution thanking him for what he had done. The arms and ammunition would be of the greatest use to the government. Hopkins could hardly have done it a greater service than in capturing them.

Of the cannon he had brought home the Admiral sent twenty-six to Newport, seven to Dartmouth and thirty-six he left at New London.

But the enthusiasm over the Admiral's cruise soon died down. Before long criticism as well as praise began to be heard. People wondered why the *Glasgow* had been allowed to escape when the whole fleet had been there to stop her. The Admiral was blamed because she had not been captured. He began to be blamed, too, for having gone down to the Bahamas at all when his orders had been to protect the southern coast. Most of all, he was criticised for the way he had placed the cannon. There was a strong feeling that he should never have given them to the smaller towns, as he had done. They should have been sent to New York and Philadelphia, and some weeks after his return Congress demanded that he should do this.

But Admiral Hopkins was not able to meet this demand. The cannon were no longer in his possession. Newport was willing to do as Congress ordered, and send on the twenty-six that had been left with her, but the Governor of Connecticut refused to give up those that were in his towns, and the feeling against the Admiral grew stronger than ever.

It was less than two months since Congress had passed a resolution thanking the Admiral for all he had done. Now it passed a resolution that was very different from that first one, for it was a resolution of censure; it declared that "the conduct of Commodore Hopkins deserves censure, and this house does accordingly censure him."

This resolution must have been a great blow to the commodore. It was a rebuke given to him before all the country. It must have been particularly hard to bear because it followed so closely after the praises he had received. His brother Stephen was so offended by it that he left Philadelphia and did not enter the city again until a year afterward.

Some good friends the Commodore still had, even in Congress, but his enemies were very bitter ones. Everything they could do to injure him they did.

Perhaps his worst enemies of all were the owners of certain armed vessels called "privateers." The vessels were called privateers because they belonged to private companies or people. The owners held letters from the government that gave their ships the right to capture any British vessels they met, whenever and however they could.

Many of the captured vessels were rich prizes. Often they were sold for a great deal of money — money that went into the pockets of the owners of the privateers, or were shared by them with their captains and seamen.

These shipowners were jealous of the navy and the prizes it took. They felt it meant just that much loss of money to them. They wished to take all the prizes themselves. They did all they could, by offering higher wages and a larger share of prize money, to make the seamen desert from the navy and serve on their privateers.

Often the Admiral's vessels lay idle and useless because he could not get men for them, while the privateers sailed up and down the waters, attacking and capturing and selling many a vessel that should have been a government prize.

Commodore Hopkins urged Congress to stop the privateering, or at least to limit it, but Congress would not move in the matter. Too many of the members were themselves owners, or part owners, of privateers. Neither would Congress do anything to restrain the captains who were taking on board their own vessels the deserters from the navy.

At one time Washington lent Hopkins two hundred and fifty men from the army to man his vessels, but some of these fell ill, others deserted, and after a short time Washington demanded that those who were left should be sent back to him, as they were needed on land.

Now and then Hopkins was able to fit out a few vessels and send them on cruises, but much of the work Congress instructed him to do he was unable to do on account of this lack of men.

His officers, too, became careless in their work. They were often disrespectful, and even disobedient, but their commander had no power to dismiss them.

As his enemies grew stronger they made several attempts to have the Commodore himself dismissed from the navy, but in this they failed, for a time at least. Instead of dismissing him, the Marine Committee paid Hopkins a great compliment. They instructed him to buy the armed schooner *Hawk* and change its name to the *Hopkins*. They also gave him the right to hoist his own flag on any and every vessel; for at that time almost every vessel in the navy carried a different flag; there was no especial one that was in use for all.

This compliment from the Marine Committee was a matter for great rejoicing among Hopkins's friends.

But their rejoicings did not last long. His enemies were still working busily against him, and in

March, 1777, they partly succeeded in what they were trying to do, for the Admiral was "suspended" from the navy. About a year later, in January, 1778, they succeeded altogether, and Commodore Hopkins was dismissed from the service.

Many of the Commodore's friends were afraid the unjust treatment he had received from the government might turn him against his country and drive him into taking part with the British, but this it never did. Hopkins was always a true and faithful patriot, and served the colonies well as long as he was able. He drilled troops, he was in the assembly, and took part in many public events.

He lived to be eighty-two years old, and died at the home farm near Providence. The old house in which he spent so much of his life is still standing, and a tablet in his honor marks it as the home of the first Commander of the American navy.[6]

The Hopkins Homestead

## NOTES

1. Esek Hopkins was born April 26, 1718, at Chapumiscook, now Chopmist, Scituate, R. I. He went to Newport in 1741, and lived there until 1755, when he removed to his farm at Providence.

2. His wife was Desire Burroughs, the daughter of one of the leading merchants of Newport.

3. These vessels were the *Alfred*, flagship, twenty-four guns, Dudley Saltonstall commanding; *Columbus*, twenty guns, Abraham Whipple commanding; *Andrea Doria*, fourteen guns, Nicholas Biddle cammanding; *Cabot*, fourteen guns, John B. Hopkins commanding; sloop *Providence* (formerly *Katy*), twelve guns, Captain Hazzard commanding; *Hornet*, ten guns; *Fly*, eight guns.

4. The *Fly* and the *Hornet* were the two vessels that were separated from the others. The *Fly* rejoined the fleet at New Providence, but the *Hornet* was not seen again during the entire cruise.

5. Among those who were severely wounded was Captain John B. Hopkins, the commander of the *Cabot*. He was a son of Admiral Hopkins.

6. The old Hopkins farm is now within the limits of the city of Providence. A part of it is used as public-school playgrounds.

Suddenly the Boy Was Filled with Shyness

How, Once Upon A Time,
A Rhode Island Boy
Became A Famous
General

Safely They Passed the British Soldiers, Nathanael Nodding to Them in Friendly Fashion

NATHANAEL GREENE was one of eight brothers. His father was a blacksmith who had a forge and mill at Warwick. The blacksmith was a Quaker, and a stern, hard-working man. He labored all day himself, and he did not see why his sons should not do the same. They had no books but the Bible or a few volumes of sermons. They had no toys nor games, but then they would have had no time to play with them, busy as they were from morning till night.

But Nathanael was a lively, high-spirited lad, and fond of fun and pleasure. Whenever he could he would steal an hour from his work, and slip away to join the other boys of the town in their games.

If it had been one of his brothers who did this, no doubt he would have been punished for it, but Nathanael was his father's favorite, and the blacksmith was more lenient with him than with the others.

None of the eight lads ever had very much schooling. Their father would have thought it a waste of time.

It was not until Nathanael was fourteen that he began to be interested in books and study.[1] He had never read much before then, but now he borrowed books wherever and whenever he could, and would sit poring over them in every spare moment, forgetful of everything around him.

But borrowing did not content him. He longed to own books of his own. He knew his father would never give him the money to buy them, so he determined to earn some money for himself.

Though Nathanael was only a boy, he was very skilful in his work, particularly at the forge. Now in his few leisure moments he began to work out a number of little toys, tiny hammers, anchors, and little play forges. Then the next time his father sent one of the older boys to Newport on business Nathanael begged to be allowed to go, too.

In the town he had no trouble in selling his toys. They were so prettily made that his father's customers were glad to buy them. The money he received for them was enough to pay for several books.

Telling his brother that he would meet him at the boat-landing later on, Nathanael hurried away to a book-shop he had seen on one of the streets. He opened the door and went in. The shop was empty except for the bookseller and a gentleman in the dress of a clergyman, who was talking to him. This gentleman was the Rev. Dr. Stiles, who was afterward the president of Yale College.[2]

Suddenly the boy was filled with shyness. He stood holding the money tightly in his hand, but was so ignorant that he did not even know what books to ask for, nor what he wanted.

Dr. Stiles pitied his confusion, and he liked the bright, honest look of the lad's face. He began to talk to him, and in such a kindly way that Nathanael soon found himself telling of how he wanted to read and study, and had earned the money for some books, and now did not know what to buy.

Dr. Stiles advised him to get "Watts' Elements of Logic," "Locke on the Human Understanding," and a copy of "Euclid."

This the boy did, and when, a little later, he left the shop he was the happy possessor of three books of his very own, books that were the beginning of what afterward grew to be a fine library.

When he reached home he set about studying these books and soon knew them almost by heart. He did not allow his reading to interfere with his work, however. Indeed he labored so hard at the forge that he became somewhat lame; a lameness that he never entirely got rid of.

It was his industry that made his father willing for him to go on with his studies, and even, later on, to take up Latin and mathematics under a master.

But in the midst of all this work and study Nathanael again began to long for some exercise and amusement. He somehow managed to learn to dance, a thing that is strictly forbidden by the Quakers. After this, many a night, while the rest of the household were sleeping, Nathanael would quietly slip from his window and hurry away to join the other young people in their frolics.

But one time, when Nathanael came home after an evening spent in dancing, he saw a dark figure pacing up and down in front of the house. It was the sturdy blacksmith, and in his hand he carried a heavy horsewhip. Nathanael at once guessed that his father had discovered his absence, and meant to punish him for it. Close by lay a pile of loose shingles. Hastily stooping down in the shadow,

Nathanael picked up several of them and slipped them in under his clothing, next to his body. Then boldly he marched forward to meet his father. As he had expected, the angry old Quaker seized him by the collar, and gave him the worst thrashing he had ever received. The whip was heavy, the blacksmith's arm was strong, but Nathanael never flinched nor made a sound. Angry as his father was, he could not but admire the lad's pluck and bravery. But the fact was that, thanks to the shingles, Nathanael never felt one of the blows that fell upon him.

This adventure put a stop to Nathanael's fun for a time, but not for long. Soon he was stealing out again at night, but never again was he caught at it.

As Nathanael grew older his father came more and more to depend on him. In 1770 he gave him entire charge of a mill at Coventry. The young man was very proud of being made a mill manager. He built himself a comfortable house on a hill overlooking the Pawtuxet River.

In this house he had a special room for his books. He had almost three hundred, and that was an unusually large library for those days.[3]

Almost all the books he bought after he came to Coventry were about the lives of great generals, or told of wars and battles. Over these books Nathanael pored as eagerly as, when a boy, he had pored over his Latin and mathematics. Often he sat up almost all night long reading them. Only toward morning would he throw himself down for an hour or two of sleep before the day's work should begin. The great battlefields and the plans of the generals grew as familiar to him as his own house and the management of the mill.

And now, too, he began to go to watch the militia drills, and to take an interest in the raising of colonial troops. This was a great offence to the Quakers, for they believed that anything that had to do with fighting was wrong. They remonstrated with him, and urged him to keep away from the drills, and when they found he would not heed them, they "read him out of meeting" — that is, they took from him all rights in their society. They would no longer allow him to belong to it.

This must have been a great sorrow to Nathanael, for he was still a Quaker in many ways, even though he did believe that in some cases the only right thing to do was to fight.

The breath of war was in all the land at this time. The American colonies were all astir with discontent and unrest. There was much talk of *independence* and *freedom from British rule*. Many men in the colonies were still loyal to the king; Tories they were called, and they wished for nothing better than to be English subjects. But there were many others who were in favor of freedom and self-government. These were called Whigs.

The feeling between the Whigs and Tories was very bitter. It was a feeling that often turned friends into enemies, and divided families with fierce quarrels.

Nathanael Greene was a Whig. He was one of the first in the country to say that the time was coming when it would be necessary for the colonies to separate from England entirely.

In 1774, four years after he came to Coventry, Nathanael married Miss Katherine Littlefield, the daughter of one of his neighbors. Soon after he married he laid aside his Quaker dress, openly declared he would be a soldier, and joined the Kentish Guards.

But he had no musket, and that was a great drawback for a soldier. A musket was a hard thing to buy in those days, too, when England had grown suspicious, and was doing her best to keep the colonists from arming.

Nathanael again put on his Quaker garb, his drab coat and broad-brimmed hat, and journeyed away to Boston. There, thanks to his dress, he was able to buy the coveted musket. Every one knew the Quakers were in favor of peace; no one could imagine that that pleasant, quiet-looking young Quaker could want a musket for shooting anything but rabbits or wild turkeys.

The purchase was made, but the next thing was how to get the musket back to Rhode Island. All about the town was the British garrison. If any one were found carrying firearms out of the town he would almost certainly be arrested, and perhaps kept a prisoner. The only thing to do was to smuggle it out of the town. Nathanael found a carter who was going his way, and induced the man to hide the musket under the straw in the bottom of the wagon. He himself mounted to the seat beside the carter and rode there, looking so peaceful in his drab coat and Quaker hat that no one thought of stopping or questioning him. Safely they passed the British soldiers, Nathanael nodding to them in friendly fashion. The cart rattled and bumped on its way. Massachusetts was left behind; the borders of Rhode Island were passed. Only then did Nathanael dare to draw out the musket from its hiding-place, examine it with joy, and feel himself at last a real soldier.

In 1775, with the first shots fired at Lexington, the struggle for independence began. Then drums were beat and flags unfurled. Through all the land sounded the tread of marching feet. Washington's army lay at Boston, and it was to join him there that the troops were marching. Not the last to set out were the Kentish Guards. They also were eager to bear their part in the struggle for freedom, and of them all none was more eager than the Quaker soldier Nathanael Greene.

But the Guards were to meet with a great disappointment: they had hardly reached the borders of Rhode Island when they received a message from the Governor telling them to come back. This Governor, a Tory, declared that not with his consent should a single shot be fired against the British forces.

The Guards complained bitterly about this order. There was even talk of disobeying the Governor and going on to Boston in spite of his commands. That was what Greene urged them to do. But in the end they decided on obedience, and turned back toward home.

Four men alone refused to turn back; these were Nathanael Greene, his brother, and two trusty friends. These four men took horse and hurried on toward Boston. Hard and fast they galloped. They hardly took time to eat or sleep, and as soon as they reached the town they made haste to offer their services to the Commander-in-chief. He should know that four Rhode Island men, at least, were willing to fight for freedom.

But after all there were other patriots in the little

state besides these four men. Not long after the return of the Kentish Guards other troops were raised, who took the name of the Army of Observation. This little army stood ready to join Washington at any time, whether the Governor should give his consent or not. Nathanael Greene was chosen to command them, with the title of Brigadier-General.

As soon as Greene heard he was appointed commander he returned to Rhode Island and set about drilling the troops. The soldiers were perfectly raw and untrained, and he himself knew but little more than they, but he worked so hard training and disciplining them that they became almost the best troops in the whole army. Washington said of them: "They are under better government than any around Boston"; and his military secretary wrote that Greene's command was "the best disciplined and appointed in the whole American army."

Washington and Greene soon became close friends. Washington depended on Greene's judgment and good sense, and Greene thought the Commander-in-chief the greatest and wisest of men. He would accept criticism and reproof from him as he would from no one else, for Greene always had a hot and unruly temper in spite of his Quaker training that made for peace.

This friendship between the Commander-in-chief and Greene made some of the other officers very jealous. They criticised Greene bitterly for many things he did and said, but it was almost always their jealousy that caused the criticisms. When the matter was examined it was generally found that Nathanael had been in the right.

In the winter of 1778-79 our army lay in camp at

Valley Forge. The sufferings of the soldiers through that winter were very great. They were poorly paid or not paid at all. They had not enough food. Their clothing fell into rags and their bare feet bled on the frozen ground. Their only beds were the earthen floors of their huts, until Washington ordered the farmers around to thrash out their grain and give the straw to the soldiers, and then they used this straw for beds. What the farmers would not do was to give the soldiers the grain and livestock they so sorely needed. The Americans were too poor to pay for the things, so the farmers preferred to sell them to the British, who gave them good money in return.

The condition of the army was miserable indeed, and at last Washington urged Greene to take the position of commissary-general. He felt Greene might perhaps do more to help them than any one else. It is the duty of a commissary to supply the troops with necessary food and clothing, and to see that they have arms and ammunition. Greene was very unwilling to give up his position as a field officer, and to take up these new duties. When at last he agreed it was only his love for Washington that made him consent.

With Greene as commissary the condition of the army became somewhat better, though there was still a great deal of suffering. He begged for help from the public and from private people. He urged Congress to vote the army money, supplies, and clothing; but Congress could do little. The whole country was poor, and there were many demands for public money.

At last the soldiers were given permission to forage

anywhere within seventy miles of Valley Forge, and take any food and livestock they could find. This frightened the farmers. They were afraid they would lose everything they had. They carried their possessions away to swamps and lonely places in the woods and hid them there.

Many of these hiding-places were found by the soldiers, however. Sometimes they would find a bag of meal hidden away in a hollow log, or a coop full of chickens in a deep thicket, or a cow or a pig. Then there would be great rejoicing in the camp.

No one was so clever at finding things as General Greene. Sometimes it almost seemed as though he could smell the meal where it lay hidden, or hear from miles away the cluck of a hen or the munching of a cow.

Mrs. Greene spent a great deal of time in the camp with her husband. Greene had never lost his love of dancing. Several times he gave dancing parties at his headquarters, to which he invited the officers and their wives. At one of these "hops" Washington was Mrs. Greene's partner, and it is said that they danced together for three hours without stopping. General Greene wrote of it afterward as "on the whole, quite a gay little frisk."

Greene finally gave up his position as commissary, but when he did so the army was already in better condition. The hardest time was passed. His enemies accused him of having made money while he was in charge of the supplies, but the fact was that when he gave up the position he was poorer than when he took it; part of what had been spent for the soldiers had been taken from his own private means.

Soon after he gave up his position as commissary-general he was appointed to the command of the army in the South, in the place of General Gates, who had been commanding it. It was in this campaign that Greene won his greatest fame, a fame that is thought by some to be even greater than that of Washington himself.

The condition of the American army in the South was very miserable. The British, under Cornwallis, were in possession of both South Carolina and Georgia. The most of the people in those states were Tories. They refused to supply our troops with food. The starving soldiers stole from the fields and orchards whenever they could, but the corn was green and the fruit not ripe. For weeks they had nothing but this green corn and fruit to eat. They were sick. Their clothing was in rags, and they were so discouraged that they felt there was nothing but defeat before them.

But Greene soon changed all this. His experience as a commissary at Valley Forge served him well. He managed to get food where there had seemed to be none before. He got them clothing and fresh ammunition. Best of all, he filled them with hope. Here was a commander, they felt, to lead them on to success, instead of the endless defeats they had suffered under Gates. Once more they laughed and joked as they sat around the campfires and talked of the victories they were to win.

But the worst thing about the Southern army was its lack of discipline. Greene found that the soldiers had been in the habit of leaving camp almost whenever they chose and without permission. They would go off to visit their families and friends, and sometimes stay away for days. He determined to put a stop to this at once and for always. He gave notice that the first man caught deserting in this way would be put to death.

It was not long before a man was brought before him who had been seen slipping off without leave. Greene gave orders for the troops to be turned out; the deserter was brought before them and shot there in the sight of all. This example of how deserters were to be punished made a deep impression on the soldiers, and at once put an end to the deserting, as Greene had intended it should.

Both the discipline and the health of his troops had now greatly improved, but Greene realized that his forces were not strong enough for him to risk an open engagement with Cornwallis. He had not enough men. But though he was weak in the number of private soldiers, he was fortunate in having with him a number of very brilliant officers: Morgan, Campbell, Sumpter, Marion, Pickens, Lee, Howard Williams, William Washington — all these were very unusual men. They knew the country well, they could understand his plans, and were able to carry them out.

Though the British were strong in the number of their men, they had comparatively few officers, and those few were not as good as Greene's. Greene decided to separate his forces into a number of small divisions, and put each division under an officer that he could absolutely depend on. With these divisions he would attack in several different places — places far apart. To meet these attacks Cornwallis would be obliged to separate his forces into a number of divisions also, and send them off in different directions. If these divisions had poor officers to command them they would be more apt to be defeated than if they were all kept together, where Cornwallis himself could direct their movements.

This plan was a brilliant piece of generalship on the part of Greene, and it succeeded even as well as he had hoped. The numbers of the British counted for little when poorly managed by their officers.

At the battle of the Cowpens the British met with one of the severest defeats of the whole campaign. The Americans, under Morgan, took more than five hundred of them prisoners. Of these, twenty-three were officers. More than a hundred British were killed, while the Americans lost, all told, only seventy men.

This victory of Morgan's was a great blow to Cornwallis. His first idea now was to pursue Morgan with the main body of his army, and get back the prisoners who had been taken. But Greene guessed that this would be the enemy's next move. It was exactly what he wished Cornwallis to do. It would give to him the chance of drawing the British away from Georgia and South Carolina, into states that were not so friendly to them.

Sending the prisoners ahead, Greene with all his forces retreated north toward Virginia, the British pursuing hotly after him. Greene was very anxious not to be caught and forced to fight. He pushed his troops on so fast that they were scarcely given time to sleep, and had only one meal a day. All through the long, bright hours and on into the night they marched and marched away toward the North. Sometimes the way lay through the deep woods or treacherous swamps; sometimes along highways and past farmhouses where the people hurried to the fences to see the ragged, dusty troops march past. Weary and footsore as the soldiers were, they were not discouraged. They joked and laughed on their way, and waved their battered caps to the country people as they passed the houses.

Late at night a halt would be called. Muskets would be thrown aside, and the weary soldiers would drop down where they stood and fall into a deep sleep. A few hours later they would be aroused by the bugles. Sometimes they had to be awakened by the officers who went about among them shaking them by their shoulders and forcing them to their feet. Still half asleep they would stumble to their feet and the march would begin again, broken at noon by a hasty meal that they swallowed down with ravenous hunger.

And all the while, close at their heels, came the British, hot to overtake them and force them into an open engagement. At one place it seemed as though the Americans must certainly be overtaken. They had reached the shore of the Catawba River and there was some difficulty in getting across. While the last of them were still in the boats on the river the British reached the bank they had just left, and made ready to embark.

Then suddenly the sky above them darkened; the wind rose, almost swamping the boats; there was a crash of thunder, and almost immediately the heavens seemed to open, and the rain poured down in a torrent. The men in the boats were half drowned, but they managed to reach the shore. Then, as suddenly as it had begun, the rain ceased, but in that little while the river had risen to a foaming torrent. It would no longer be possible to cross it until it had gone down.

The British commanders were filled with helpless rage. They had thought that at last they were on the point of overtaking the Americans, but this delay would give them a fresh start. And, indeed, by the time Cornwallis could cross the river Greene was again in advance, and a few days later he crossed the Dan into Virginia, where he was safe.

Now at last the weary American troops could rest for a time and eat and sleep, for Virginia was friendly territory. The gaunt and weary soldiers grew strong on the good fare. They were joined by reinforcements and their ammunition was replenished.

It was now the British who were in a dangerous position. They had been drawn away from the states that were friendly to them and were among enemies. The men were worn out with their forced marches, and for them there were no reinforcements.

It was on the 13th of February that Greene's forces had crossed the Dan into Virginia. Ten days afterward he brought his troops, rested and refreshed, back into North Carolina again. But he did not settle them in one place. Instead, he changed his place of encampment at least twice in every twenty-four hours, and kept the British constantly anxious and harassed because they never knew where the Americans were nor when they might make an attack. Greene, on the other hand, was never ignorant for even three hours of exactly where the British were.

Cornwallis began to see that unless he had some sudden stroke of good fortune he was doomed to defeat. He longed to meet the Americans in open battle before his forces grew any weaker, but he was obliged to wait for Greene's own choice of time and place.

The engagement between the two forces at last took place at Guilford Courthouse. It was one of the fiercest of all the battles in the War for Independence. On both sides there were heavy losses, but the British fought with the fury of desperate men, and the Americans were at last driven back and forced to retreat.

But their seeming defeat was really better than a victory for the Americans. The British had lost so many men and were so weakened that they dared not stay where they were, nor did they dare to try to return to South Carolina. Cornwallis gave up all possession of the two southern states he had held and that he had hoped to keep out of the Union. Greene went north and rejoined Washington.

South Carolina and Georgia were so grateful to Greene for what he had done in freeing them from the British that they each presented him with a valuable tract of land.

For two years after the close of the war General Greene lived in Rhode Island, doing all he could to bring about a friendly feeling between the Whigs and Tories, for they were still very bitter toward each other. Only time, however, could quiet down this feeling between them and bring peace to the country.

At the end of two years Greene took his family down to the beautiful place near Savannah that Georgia had given to him. Here he hoped to live happily and see his children grow up about him.

But it was only for a very short time that he enjoyed it. One hot day, as he was crossing the garden, he was suddenly overcome by the heat of the sun, and fell down, insensible.

He was carried to the house, doctors were sent for, and everything possible was done to save him. But it was all of no use, and two days later he died.

The news of his death filled the whole country with mourning. At Savannah the bells of the city were tolled. Shops were closed, all business stopped, and the flags, even those on the ships in the harbor, were lowered to half-mast.

To Washington the blow was indeed a heavy one. Greene had been his close and dear friend. He had loved and trusted him as he loved and trusted few others. The grief of Greene's family was bitter, but perhaps Washington, even more than they, had been able to appreciate the wisdom, the bravery, and the true patriotism of the son of the Warwick blacksmith.

Still Half Asleep, They Would Stumble to Their Feet and the March Would Begin Again

## NOTES

1. His interest was first aroused by his making the acquaintance of a lad named Giles, who was a student at Rhode Island College, now Brown University.

2. Dr. Stiles was himself a Quaker. Later on he visited Friend Greene at Warwick, and it was he who induced the stern old Quaker to allow his son to study Latin and mathematics under a master.

3. Greene always seemed to feel a sort of awe toward those who had the advantages of an early education. He always felt his own lack of it very bitterly. We find him, in one of his letters to his wife, urging her to be careful about her spelling.

4. Greene finally gave up the position in a fit of exasperation at Congress because they would do so little and were so slow in voting supplies for the army.

Then They Sprang to Their Feet with a Yell and Poured a Fierce Volley in Among the Redcoats

# How, Once Upon A Time, The Battle Of Rhode Island Was Fought

The People on the Island Hurried to the Cliffs

IT WAS the year 1776, and the war with England had begun. Along the roads sounded the rumble of artillery and the tramp of armed troops.

In December a squadron of British vessels sailed into Newport Harbor; the troops landed and took possession of the town.

On the mainland people were terrified lest the British should come there, too. Those living near the coast were advised to send their women and children back into the country for safety, and their furniture and cattle as well. For a time the roads were almost blocked with loaded carts, and with droves of cattle and flocks of sheep. The militia armed and prepared to defend their state, and besides the militia enough volunteers enlisted to make a full regiment themselves.

Messengers were hurriedly sent to the other New England States to ask for aid, and Massachusetts and Connecticut almost at once sent troops. It was indeed very important for all of New England that Rhode Island should be protected. Rhode Island had sixty miles of coastline, at any point of which the British might land unless there were troops to defend it, and her shores were like an open door to the rest of the country.

In 1777 General Spencer was in command of the Rhode Island forces, and in October of that year he determined to try to drive the British from Newport and the island. This plan was highly approved by Congress. A force of about 9,000 troops was gathered together to make the attack. The British had scarcely 4,000, but their position was very strong.

The Americans would be obliged to cross to the island in boats. The time for this was decided on; the troops were ready, and all the preparations seemed to have been made, but when the time came for the soldiers to embark it was found there were not enough boats to carry them across. This was very discouraging. The expedition had to be put off. A heavy storm came up and swept the coast, and the men began to desert. Soon the American forces were so weakened that all plans for crossing to the island were given up.

General Spencer was severely blamed for this failure, and the feeling against him was so strong that in December he gave up his command.

His place was taken by Major John Sullivan.[1]

Sullivan was a brave and daring officer, and a close friend of both Washington and Nathanael Greene.

Soon after he took command[2] he began to plan to carry out the attack on the British that Spencer had given up. He applied to Congress for more troops, and in June all of the Rhode Island troops that were in the Continental Army were sent back to their own state.

The British had learned of Sullivan's plans, and determined to do what they could to interrupt them. An expedition was sent out to destroy some boats that were in the Kickemuit River. After destroying the boats the enemy attacked the towns of Warren and Bristol. Nineteen buildings in Bristol were

## THE BATTLE OF RHODE ISLAND

burned, houses were looted, and a number of people were carried off as prisoners. The British took from the houses not only arms, provisions, and furniture, but necklaces, jewels, aprons, and handkerchiefs — anything that seemed to them of value. Ladies were forced to draw the rings from their fingers and hand them over to the soldiers. Even the buckles were torn from their shoes and carried off. The soldiers afterward went about the Newport streets offering the things for sale to any one who would buy them. The prisoners who were taken were treated with such cruelty that Sullivan wrote a letter of bitter reproach to the British General Pigot. In his letter he declared that the whole expedition had been "darkened with savage cruelty, and stained with indelible disgrace."

At this time the French were our allies.[3] Lafayette had come over to join the American army and fight in the cause of liberty. A French fleet under the command of the Comte D'Estaing had been sent to help us. It had been lying in the neighborhood of New York, but in July it set sail for Rhode Island[4] to aid the American forces there. This was good news for Sullivan. There were troops on board who would strengthen his forces on land, and the vessels could protect him on the water-side.

The British, on the other hand, heard the news with great anxiety. They strengthened still further the defences they had on the island. Forts were rebuilt and earthworks thrown up, and reinforcements were sent that raised the number of troops on the island to almost 7,000. Sullivan had only 1,600, but the number was growing. Lafayette, with two brigades, was sent to join him. Patriots from Bristol, Warren, and Providence volunteered and came marching to the front. Artillery rumbled heavily along the roads, raising a cloud of dust. Through the dust bayonets glistened in the sunlight as the troops swung past to the sound of fife and drum.

A regiment of negroes was raised, the first black regiment that was ever formed in America. Later they were to show how fiercely and faithfully they could fight. They were Rhode Island slaves, but as soon as they enlisted they were set free. These troops were raised and commanded by a Rhode Island man, James M. Varnum.

On July 29th a number of sail were sighted on the horizon toward the southeast. The people on the island hurried to the cliffs on the seaward side, and stood watching eagerly the approach of the vessels. It was impossible, however, to tell what vessels they were even when they came near, for they showed no flags. They might be either British or French.

By one o'clock the fleet had reached the mouth of the main channel, just off Point Judith, and here they dropped their sails and came to anchor. It was a magnificent sight as the great vessels lay there, rocking gently to the long swell of the water. There were twelve ships of the line, four frigates, and a corvette. Suddenly there was a flutter of white at the mastheads. The flags were being run up. A moment later they lifted in the wind, and all could see the Three Lilies of France on their white ground. It was the French fleet, our allies, and the hearts of the Americans rose high with hope as they saw those flags of the friendly nation.

The day after the arrival of the fleet Sullivan went to the flagship to talk over the plan of attack with

## THE BATTLE OF RHODE ISLAND

D'Estaing. It was decided to make the attack as soon as possible. To wait would only be to give the British a chance to strengthen their position still further. The American forces were to cross from Tiverton to the north end of the island. The French troops[4] were to land on Conanicut Island and cross from there. Meanwhile, two ships of the line, two frigates, and the corvette were to take up such a position as to keep the British ships that were in the harbor from escaping.

The movements of the French fleet were carefully watched by the British. They soon realized that their vessels were being shut in by the French, and rather than run the risk of having them captured they destroyed them. Three vessels that were in Sakonnet River were blown up. Four frigates and a corvette were run up on the beach of Rhode Island and burned. Others were burned in the harbor, and their hulks were sunk[5] there so as to obstruct navigation.

The 10th of August was the day set for the French and Americans to land on the island. Sullivan's forces had grown until now he had under him almost 10,000 troops, but the most of these were raw and untried, and had never been in battle before. Almost all of the British were veterans. However, the French, too, were tried troops, and Sullivan counted largely on them. He was full of hopes of success.

But a bitter disappointment awaited him. The French troops were landed on Conanicut as he and D'Estaing had agreed, but hardly had this been done when a British fleet was sighted down the bay. D'Estaing at once decided to reëmbark his men and sail down to meet the enemy and give battle. His troops were ordered back to the vessels, and as soon as they were on board he set sail. Sullivan knew nothing of this sudden change of plan. He was still counting on his allies, when, looking out over the water, he saw with amazement that the French fleet was disappearing in the distance.

The disappointment was so great that a feeling of discouragement spread through the whole army. Men and officers alike began to doubt whether the French were faithful to them. Lafayette was deeply mortified.

But in spite of the desertion of the fleet Sullivan determined to carry out his attack. But on the 12th of August a great storm arose that swept both land and sea. The wind blew a hurricane, and the rain fell in torrents. Arms and ammunition were made useless. It would have been impossible even for troops to march in such a storm. Tents were blown down or carried away by the wind. The soldiers were left without shelter. They crouched in the corners of fences or against rocks, trying in vain to protect themselves. Many died from the exposure.

On the sea the fleets were scattered almost before their battle had begun. Masts were broken and rigging torn away.

By the 15th the storm had passed, and during that day the French fleet again came in sight and took up the position they had held before. Sullivan hoped that now, at last, they would carry out their agreement. Instead D'Estaing sent him a message that he would have to sail to Boston to have his vessels repaired.[6] It was in vain that Sullivan urged

# THE BATTLE OF RHODE ISLAND 147

and entreated him to remain. Lafayette added his entreaties to Sullivan's, but the French admiral was determined to go to Boston. He would promise nothing except that he would return as soon as possible, and with despair Sullivan saw the sails set and the whole fleet go sweeping out past the British batteries and away toward the north.

The second desertion by the French had an even worse effect on the American forces than the first. They began to desert in large numbers. Almost 3,000 of them left and went back to the mainland, and Sullivan's force of 10,000 was reduced to 7,000.

He still held a place on the island, but with such a weakened army he dared not stay so near the enemy, and he retreated to the fortified hills at the north. He hoped it would not be long before the fleet returned, but meanwhile his heavy stores and baggage were sent to the rear where it would be easy to transport them to the mainland if this proved necessary.

By the 28th the last of the heavy baggage was carried to the rear. All was ready for a retreat, but still Sullivan waited, hoping each day that the French fleet would return, but each day he was disappointed.

On the 28th Lafayette started for Boston to try to hasten the return of the fleet. Hr crossed to the mainland and then made the journey on horseback. He was so eager to return that he made the whole journey (a distance of almost seventy miles) in less than fourteen hours.

The British had learned, with fresh hope, that Sullivan was making ready to retreat to the mainland. They determined to make an attack at once, and before his forces could leave the island.

Very early, almost with the dawning of the 29th, the British forces were on the march, and at nine their cannon opened fire on the American outworks. The heavy booming seemed to shake the island and could be heard far over on the mainland.

There were two principal highways along the island, one to the east and one to the west. Along these roads the British columns moved to the attack.

The Americans had made ready to meet them.

Two light corps had been sent out, one down the east road, and one down the west road, to meet the advance of the enemy.

A number of pickets were stationed at a crossroad that branched off from the east road. Here a field had a stone wall around it.[7] The order for these pickets was to lie concealed behind the wall until the British were close upon them, and then to fire on them and retreat. This order was well carried out.

The light corps, when attacked, fell back to the main body of the army. The order to do this was brought them by a regiment that Sullivan sent out to protect their retreat.

The pickets still crouched concealed behind the stone wall. The field lay still and peaceful in the sunlight. For a time the pickets heard nothing but the distant roar of the cannon, and the nearer volleys of artillery. The American troops had fallen back. Then from down the east road came the steady tramp of the British as they came swinging on, their bayonets glittering in the sunlight.

When they reached the crossroad there was a sharp command from their officer, and the Twenty-

## THE BATTLE OF RHODE ISLAND 149

second Regiment divided. One half of it continued along the main road, the other turned off toward the field where the Americans were concealed. Pickets still crouched there, gripping their guns and scarcely breathing. Not until the British were abreast of them did they move. Then they sprang to their feet with a yell, and poured a fierce volley in among the redcoats.

The British were so utterly unprepared that they made no attempt to return the fire. Many of them had fallen and lay groaning in the dust of the road. Before those who were unhurt could recover, the Americans had reloaded, and had again poured a storm of bullets in among the enemy. Almost one quarter of the whole Twenty-second Regiment lay there, dead or dying.

Two troops of Hessians hurried on to the support of the British, but they arrived too late. The Americans had already gone.

They had retreated to the main army without the loss of a single man.

Along the west road the fighting had been hot and furious. Twice the British and Hessians had charged upon the American regiments, and twice they had been driven back. A third attack might have had a different ending, for the American forces were almost exhausted, but two fresh battalions were sent forward by Sullivan and saved the day for them.

Varnum's regiment of negroes had been posted in a valley. It was against these that the Hessians made their fiercest attack. Three times they charged down the hill, and three times they were driven back. Though many of the blacks were killed or wounded, they had no thought of quitting their position. But the Hessians had suffered far more terribly. So many of them were killed, indeed, that the next day their officer refused to lead them. He was afraid they would shoot him for making them lose so many men. The whole battle had been a slaughter for the British forces. At one place as many as sixty Hessians were found lying dead in a heap together.

The British were forced to fall back, and the Americans pursued them hotly almost up to their fortifications. One of their batteries on Quaker Hill was captured.

Sullivan was very anxious to carry on his attack still further, but his men were too exhausted. For thirty-six hours they had been on the march, or fighting and working, without a moment to rest or eat. He was obliged to fall back to his camp and allow his troops some time for food and sleep.

On the 30th Lafayette returned from Boston, exhausted from his journey. He was bitterly disappointed when he found the battle had been fought while he was away, and a victory won. Through all that day there was some firing between the two forces, but no regular attack by either side.

Lafayette had brought a letter to Sullivan from the French admiral. In this letter D'Estaing told Sullivan that his fleet was still undergoing repairs, and that he would not be able to return for some time. Sullivan also, that same day, received a letter from Washington warning him that the British fleet, under Lord Howe, had sailed for Rhode Island, and might arrive there at any time.

This was serious news for Sullivan. If the British fleet arrived while he was still on the island and the land forces again attacked him, it would mean an

## THE BATTLE OF RHODE ISLAND 151

utter defeat of his forces, and a heavy loss. It was now very necessary for him to retreat to the mainland as quickly as possible.

To deceive the British, and make them think he still meant to hold his position, he had a number of tents brought forward and set up where the British could see them. He also set his men to work fortifying the camp. While this was going on at the front his stores and baggage were being quietly sent down to the river. Lafayette had missed the battle, but now he could do good service in helping on the withdrawal.

There was, fortunately, no moon that night. As soon as it was dark the Americans were on the move. In perfect silence troop after troop marched down to the river and embarked, and were carried over to the mainland. What was left of the stores and baggage were taken with them. It was a masterly retreat. All was done in perfect order, in perfect silence, and without a single mishap.

All night long the British sentries paced back and forth, giving the sign and countersign, and never once did they guess that the enemy they were guarding against had left the island; that their fortifications lay empty and deserted. Only as the morning light spread palely over the island did the British see that no one was left in the American camp. The enemy they had still hoped to capture had escaped them. They still held the island, indeed — in that far Sullivan had failed — but their forces had suffered a heavy defeat. They had lost 1,023 men in the battle, while the loss of the Americans was only 211.

Congress passed a vote of thanks to Sullivan for

the way he had managed the campaign. It also passed a resolution in which it said his retreat had been "prudent, timely, and well conducted." It was, indeed, a brilliant end to a brilliant victory, and Lafayette declared the Battle of Rhode Island to be "the best-fought action of the war."

The British In Newport

## NOTES

1. The father and mother of General Sullivan were Irish. They came to this country as emigrants in 1723. Their third son, John (General Sullivan), was born at Berwick, Maine, the 17th of February, 1740.

2. General Sullivan's headquarters were at Providence. The principal part of the Continental troops that were under his command were posted in this town.

3. "Early in this year (1778) the Americans were inspired with fresh hope, and animated by intelligence of the conclusion of treaties of friendship and commence an alliance with the King of France. This was an event to which they had been anxiously looking as the only thing required to give complete triumph to their cause." — "The Library of American Biography."

4. D'Estaing had first planned to enter the harbor of New York and attack the British fleet that was lying there, but he was told the water was not deep enough for his largest vessels. He was therefore obliged to give up his plan, and turned his attention to Rhode Island instead. The French troops numbered 4,000.

5. By the sinking and destroying of these vessels the British lost 212 guns.

6. D'Estaing explained that these were his orders, that in case of any disaster to his vessels he was to sail at once to Boston Harbor for repairs.

7. Near the Gibbs farm. The Union Meeting-house now stands at the southeast angle of this field.

Stuart Began upon the President's Portrait

How, Once Upon A Time,
A Rhode Island Boy
Became A Famous
Painter

Gilbert and His Sister

UPON the banks of the Pettaquamscutt River, in North Kingstown, there stands an old shingled house with a "hip" roof. It is shaded by great willow trees, and so close to the river that you can see the reflection of it in the smoothly flowing water. Within are low-ceilinged rooms, broad fireplaces, and quaint, narrow stairways.

It was in the northeast chamber of this house that a baby boy was born in December of the year 1755.

He was a very welcome little baby. His father and mother had already had two children, a boy and a girl, but of these two the boy had died, and only the girl was left.

Gilbert Stuart was the name of the father, and Gilbert Stuart this second little son was christened a few months later. He was a strong, large, sturdy child, and his parents were very proud of him.

As he grew older he became rather spoiled and wilful, for his mother could refuse him nothing: his father indulged him almost as much as his mother did, and his little sister was never tired of playing with him and keeping him amused.

Mr. Stuart was a snuff manufacturer. His snuff mill stood close to the river and only a little distance from the house. At that time a great deal of snuff was used in New England, and large orders for it were sent over to Scotland. Mr. Stuart, who was a Scotchman, had come to America hoping to make a fortune by grinding snuff here. But for some reason his business was not a success. He lost money instead of making it. After a while he and his family had little to depend on, except some money that Mrs. Stuart had inherited from her father. Luckily this was enough to support them all, but they were obliged to be very economical: there was not a dollar to waste.

When Gilbert was about twelve years old Mr. Stuart decided to remove to Newport. His mill was no longer of value to him, and he wished to be where there were schools for his children.

The children were delighted at the thought of this change. It seemed to them it would be great fun to live in a town where there were other boys and girls. They felt very little regret over leaving the softly flowing river, the trees and mill, and the old gambrel-roofed house where they had been born.

Very soon after the family settled in Newport Gilbert was entered as a pupil at a boys' school kept by the Rev. George Bissett. So far his sister had been almost his only playmate and she had always been ready to give way to him in everything; now he was to be with other boys who had their own games and sports, and were, perhaps, just as fond of having their own way as he was. It might have been supposed that at first he would have had a hard time among these new playmates, but instead he became very popular. He was so clever, so strong and handsome, and so fond of mischief that they were quite ready to allow him to be their leader.

# A FAMOUS PAINTER

He was not fond of study, but he learned quickly and easily, and generally stood well in his classes, and Mr. Bissett forgave him many a piece of mischief that he might not have forgiven to a duller or less likable boy.

One study there was, however, that Gilbert cared for almost as much as he did for his sports and games, and that was his drawing. At home he was never happier than when he had a piece of crayon or charcoal in his hand and was making pictures.

One day Dr. John Hunter came to the house to see Mrs. Stuart, who was not very well. He was much interested in some drawings of animals that Gilbert had just finished.

"Some day you must come to my house, my lad," he said, "and see two Spanish dogs I have."

Gilbert was delighted with this invitation and readily agreed to go. The time set for this visit was the next election day, as that would be a holiday.

When election day came Gilbert started off bright and early for his visit. Dr. Hunter showed him the dogs, and then put before him a canvas, palette, brushes, and colors. "Now, my boy, let me see what sort of a picture you can make of my dogs," he said.

Gilbert set about the work, and the picture was such a success that the doctor was delighted. This painting of Dr. Hunter's dogs was the first oil painting that young Stuart ever attempted. He was then about thirteen years old.

The next year he painted the portraits of Mrs. Christian Bannister and John Bannister, and the Bannisters were so pleased with them that they had them framed, and they now hang in the Redwood Library at Newport.

Stuart's drawing master at this time was Mr. Cosmos Alexander. Mr. Alexander was very proud of his pupil's work, and often declared that some day the boy would become famous, and that it was a great pity he could not study abroad. Mr. Alexander was a Scotchman, and after he had been in this country for some years he decided to return to Scotland. He was very anxious to take his pupil with him, and Gilbert was equally eager to go. He was at this time a young man of eighteen, handsome, tall, well built, and with a frank and charming manner that won the liking of every one who met him.

His parents were very unwilling, at first, to have him go so far from them, but Gilbert urged and pleaded so eagerly that at last they gave their consent.

Mrs. Stuart wept bitterly over parting with her son, but the young man was full of high hopes. He meant to make a name for himself and to win fame and money before he returned.

He was away for two years. Of what happened in those two years his parents knew very little. Gilbert was never one to write or talk of disagreeable things if he could help it, but very unhappy times he must have had in the months he was away, for one day he suddenly appeared at home, thin, ragged, and forlorn.

His parents could hardly believe their eyes when he walked in. They had thought he was still in Scotland. They questioned him as to what had happened, and why he had returned so suddenly, but they could learn little from him. He told them Mr. Alexander had died, leaving him in the care of a friend; that he had wanted to come home but had had no money to pay for a passage, so had worked his way back on a collier. More than this he would not tell them.

But, whatever had happened, Mrs. Stuart was only too thankful to have her son at home again. His father for his part was pleased to see that the young man had learned at least one thing while he was away, and that was to work. A blacksmith was hired as a model, and young Stuart set to work eagerly, drawing, painting, scraping out what he had done if it was not good and painting it over again.

Before long he again began to be talked about as a promising young artist. His uncle, Captain Joseph Anthony, decided to have him paint Mrs. Anthony and the children, and the portraits were such a success that Captain Anthony paid his nephew well for them.

Stuart was delighted at having earned something at last, but the money was soon spent. Neither then nor at any other time did he seem to have any idea of saving or being economical. Whatever he earned was spent almost before he received it, and he did not seem to know how it had gone.

There were many wealthy Jews in Newport at this time, and several of them ordered portraits from Stuart and paid him even more liberally than his uncle had. It seemed as though there were a fine opening for the young artist there in his own town.

But now great events began to happen that changed all the plans Stuart had been making. It was the year 1775 and the country was in a turmoil. Drums were beaten, speeches made, and men were mustered in as soldiers. It was the beginning of the

Revolutionary War, that was to make the American colonies into an independent country. But Gilbert had no taste for war. What he wanted was peace and quiet, that he might work undisturbed.

Moreover, he needed to earn a living, and he soon found that people had now neither thoughts nor money to spend on having their portraits painted. They were busy with greater things. He determined to go abroad again, and not to return until these troublous times were over. So on June 16th, the very day before the Battle of Bunker Hill was fought, he once more said good-bye to his family and set sail, but this time for England instead of Scotland.

There was an artist living in London at this time, Sir Benjamin West, who had gone there from Philadelphia and had made himself famous by his paintings. It was the great ambition of most of the young American painters to study under West. So as soon as Gilbert landed in England he made his way at once to London, hoping to get an introduction to the great painter.

But after he reached there, for some reason or other, he did not try to see West. Perhaps he was ashamed to go to him poor and ragged: for Stuart had again spent all his money. He was in actual poverty, without enough even to pay for food and clothing or for the garret where he lived.

He was almost in despair, when chance threw a piece of good fortune in his way. He was passing a church one day when he heard a sound of music. He pushed open the door and went in and sat down in one of the pews. A number of young men were sitting in the front of the church and one after another they went to the organ and played something. Stuart soon found that the church needed an organist, and these young men were trying for the position. He, too, asked to be allowed to play, and he did so much better than any of the others that the judges at once chose him to be the organist. The salary was to be thirty pounds a year: that is about $150. Stuart was filled with joy over this lucky chance. He had been so absolutely without money that a hundred and fifty dollars seemed to him a fortune. He at once had a good meal and bought himself some clothes. Soon, however, he had spent almost all of the money that had been advanced to him, and had scarcely enough left to buy food to keep him from starving.

But now he had another stroke of good fortune. An old friend of his, Dr. Waterhouse, came to live in London. He heard that Stuart was there and at once hunted him up. He was shocked to find the painter living in a miserable garret without enough to eat or wear, and in debt for the little he had.

Dr. Waterhouse paid his debts, lent him some money, and made him move to a more comfortable place. He also managed to get for him some orders for portraits.

It seemed as though all would now be well with the young painter, but instead of setting to work upon the orders he had received Stuart only idled away his time. Some of the work he put off from day to day. Some portraits he began and then laid aside because he was not satisfied with them. He seemed to prefer to borrow money from Waterhouse rather than earn it for himself.

If it had been any one but Stuart who acted in this way his friend would, no doubt, have grown tired of helping him and have told him to shift for himself, but the painter was so gay, and charming, and talented that all through his life his friends seemed willing to forgive him anything.

It was not until two years after he reached London that Stuart made up his mind to go to see West. He dressed himself in a new suit and a fashionable overcoat, which he had just bought with some borrowed money, and made his way to the painter's house and asked to see him.

Like every one else, West was charmed with the young Rhode Islander. After talking to him and examining his work, West readily agreed to take him as a pupil: and not only that, he even invited Stuart to come and live with him in his own house for as long as he would.[1]

This was a great thing for Stuart. There was perhaps little that West could teach him, for his own style of painting was already better than that of his master, but he was forced to work more steadily now that he had some one over him, and through West he met some of the greatest artists and most famous men in London. It was by his master's advice, too, that he went to lectures given by Sir Joshua Reynolds.

One of the most important picture exhibitions in London is that of the Royal Academy. It is the great ambition of every young artist to have a picture hung in it.

In 1777 Stuart was given an order to paint a portrait of Mr. William Grant, a Scotchman. The first day that Mr. Grant came to pose for the picture it was very cold. He happened to say that it was much better weather for skating than for sitting. Stuart at once laid aside his palette and brushes and suggested that they should go out and skate on the Serpentine River. Mr. Grant agreed, and they started out together. The Scotchman was a good skater, but Stuart was a better. While they were out in the middle of the river the ice around them began to crack. The painter bade his companion take hold of his coat tails, and he would soon bring him safely to the shore. This he did.

When, the next day, he began on the portrait he represented Mr. Grant as skating on the Serpentine. The picture was a great success. It was offered to the Royal Academy, and was at once accepted and hung in one of the best positions. Crowds gathered before it to look at it, and the young painter found himself famous.

He now decided to have a house and studio of his own, and of this West greatly approved. When West bade his pupil good-bye he said: "Stuart, you have done well, very well; now all you have to do is go home and *do better*."

The young painter's house soon became very popular. He was so gay and amusing that people were always glad to come to see him, and besides that he was growing more and more famous. He had more orders than he could possibly find time for, and he asked very high prices for his work. He spent his money as though there would never be any end to it, and he was so careless that often he did not know whether a picture had been paid for or not.

When he was about thirty Stuart fell in love with Miss Charlotte Coates, the daughter of an English doctor. She was a beautiful girl, and she sang extremely well. Stuart himself was very musical.

Though the painter was popular and famous, Miss Coates's family was very unwilling to have her marry him. They knew what a spendthrift he was, and feared that he might bring her to poverty in spite of the large sums of money he was making.

However, she was in love with him and determined to marry him, and the wedding took place on May 10, 1786.

The young Mrs. Stuart was almost as fond of pleasure and gayety as her husband, and they gave so many fine entertainments, and spent money so freely, that it was not very long before they found they were in debt. Stuart's pictures were still famous, and the people still paid large sums for them, but the money was spent before it came in.

The debts grew heavier and heavier, and at last the Stuarts decided to leave London and go to live in Dublin. They hoped to be able to live more cheaply there, where they would not have so many friends.

But in Dublin it proved no easier to live cheaply than it had in London. They were soon in debt again, and people were dunning them for money. Stuart now wished to return to America and try his fortune there, but he was so poor he did not have the money to pay for the passage for himself and his wife. However, he found a sea captain who was willing to take them back in his ship in return for a portrait which Stuart was to paint for him.

The Stuarts landed in New York, and took a house there instead of going back to Rhode Island. They soon became as popular in New York as they had been in London and Dublin; the most famous people in the city came to Stuart to have their portraits painted, and he soon had all the work he could do. He began many portraits, however, that were never finished. If he was not satisfied with the work he put it aside, and nothing would induce him to go on with it. There were dozens of unfinished portraits in the garret of his house.

Stuart had a very quick temper, and never could bear to be criticised. Once, when he was painting a lady, she rose from her seat, and came and looked over his shoulder, and made some criticism on the likeness. The artist managed to answer pleasantly, and for a few minutes he went on with his painting, fighting to keep down his temper. Then suddenly he rose, put down his brushes, and took the picture from the easel. "Excuse me, madam," he said, "but I cannot paint by direction."

"But at least you will finish the picture?" cried the lady in dismay.

"No, I cannot work on it any more," answered Stuart.

The lady begged and implored him to forgive her, and go on with the picture; she even wept, but Stuart refused to touch it again. It was carried away and stored in the garret with the rest of his unfinished work, and the unhappy lady never saw it again.

Soon after Stuart was settled in New York the Duke of Kent sent him word that he wished to have his portrait painted, and offered to send a warship for Stuart if he would return to England to do it, but the painter refused. He was at this very time anxious to paint a portrait of George Washington. Indeed, it was said that he had come back to America for that especial purpose. He would not leave the country again until he had done it. He thought General Washington was the greatest man of his times.

It was not until the winter of 1794, however, that Stuart went to Philadelphia to meet the President. Generally the painter was ready enough to talk, but when finally he found himself in the same room with Washington he was so overcome with awe that he hardly dared open his lips or say a word. If the President had not already heard from others how witty and talented Stuart was he must have thought him a dull fellow indeed.

However, the sittings were arranged for, and in the spring of 1795 Stuart began upon the President's portrait. The first attempt he made was not a success. Perhaps he was still too much in awe of Washington to be at ease, or able to put his best work on it. At any rate he grew so discouraged that he refused to let any one see what he was doing, and finally he told people he had rubbed it all out.

He afterward painted two other portraits of Washington that seem to have pleased him better. One was painted for the Marquis of Lansdowne; the other is in the Museum of Fine Arts in Boston.

When the city of Washington became the capital of the United States Stuart and his family moved there, and later they went to live in Roxbury, one of the suburbs of Boston. While he was in Roxbury he painted portraits of many of the best-known people of Boston.

A list of portraits made by Stuart after he came back to America would include at least eight hundred paintings. Among them are great names: Thomas Jefferson, Mr. and Mrs. Paul Revere, Mr. and Mrs.

John Adams, Madame Bonaparte, John Jacob Astor and many others.

In 1825 Stuart's health began to fail. His hand grew so tremulous that he could hardly place the colors on the canvas. He grew very sad and depressed, and only now and then did he show flashes of the wit and gayety that had once made him so charming.

He died in July, 1828, and instead of bringing his body back to Rhode Island it was buried in the cemetery of Boston Common.

But though Stuart's grave is in Boston, and though so much of his life was spent away from Rhode Island, it was in Rhode Island that he was born, and it is Rhode Island that can claim as her son this great painter.

Gilbert Stuart's Old Home

## NOTE

1. It was not an unusual thing, at this time, for masters to take their pupils to live with them in their own houses.

"We Have Met the Enemy and They Are Ours"

How, Once Upon A Time,
A Rhode Island Man
Became The Hero
Of Lake Erie

Perry Leaving the "Lawrence" for the "Niagara"

OLIVER HAZARD PERRY went to sea as a midshipman when he was only twelve years old. The deck of the ship was his school and his playground.

The trees he climbed were the tall, stark masts of the vessels, and instead of the rustle of the leaves he heard only the rattle of the rigging and the flap of the sails.

Oliver loved the sea and the navy and rose steadily in the service.[1] When only nineteen he was a lieutenant in command of the *Nautilus* on the Mediterranean. Before he was twenty-four he had served in the war with Tripoli under Preble, and had also been master of the *Revenge* and commander of a fleet of seventeen gunboats, and had made himself known as a brave and capable officer.

Our second war with England — the "Second War for Independence," as it was called — began in the summer of 1812. Some of the most important naval battles of that war were fought on the great lakes of Erie and Ontario. Those lakes cover almost five hundred miles of boundary between the United States and Canada. It was from Canada that the British threatened to invade the Northwestern States, and so the possession of the Great Lakes was very important both to them and to the Americans. From the lakes the gunboats could aid and protect the land forces of either side, and across them the transports could carry troops and provisions far more easily than they could be sent by land.

At the outbreak of the war the Americans had only one war-brig, the *Oneida,* on the lakes, but a number of merchant vessels were at once fitted out as warships and put under the command of Captain Isaac Chauncey. These vessels were only for the protection of Lake Ontario, but orders were also given for another squadron to be built at Presque Isle, now Erie, for the defence of Lake Erie. Captain Perry was appointed commander of this fleet.

At the time of his appointment Perry was in command of a fleet in Narragansett Bay. He was ordered to send the best men from these vessels to Presque Isle and he himself was to report at once to Chauncey at Sackett's Harbor.

Perry immediately sent fifty picked men off on sledges to the northwest, and only twenty-four hours after he received the order he himself was on his way to Lake Ontario. With him he took his little brother, only thirteen years old. The weather was bitterly cold, a heavy snow lay on the ground, and the whole journey was made in a sleigh, with relays of horses.

He reached Sackett's Harbor the 3d of March, made his report to Chauncey, and was at once sent on to Presque Isle[2] to hasten the building of his squadron[3] there.

The building of this fleet was one of the remarkable feats of the war. The shipbuilders came all the way from Philadelphia and New York through an almost trackless wilderness, where they had never been before. The guns and ammunition and necessary furnishings for the vessels were brought from hundreds of miles away on sleds or slow ox-carts over difficult, almost impassable roads. Plowshares horseshoes, axe-heads, everything in iron that could be gathered together was melted up to make the bars and braces and rivets for the ships. And in less than six months after the lumber was standing untouched in the forest the vessels were finished and floating free upon the waters at the mouth of Cascade Creek, where they had been built. The vessels were finished at last and floated there stout and staunch. Arms and ammunition had been put on board. Their commander was ready and eager to sail out and meet the British, but the squadron lay idle and useless. There were not enough men to man the vessels.

Perry was in despair. He wrote to Chauncey "The enemy's fleet of six sails are now off the bar of this harbor . . . Give me men and I'll acquire, both for you and myself, glory and honor, or perish in the attempt." Again he wrote: "The enemy are within striking distance, my vessels ready and not enough men to man them." And again "For God's sake and yours and mine, send me men and I will have them all (the British vessels) in a day or two. Commodore Barclay, the British Commander, keeps just out of reach of our gunboats . . . I long to be at him. Think of my situation the enemy in sight, and yet obliged to bite my fingers with vexation for want of men."

Finally men were sent, but instead of the trained seamen Perry had hoped for they were "a motley set, blacks and soldiers and boys." Very few of them had had any experience in seamanship. Still such as they were Perry determined to set out with them

He was too eager to engage with the British to wait any longer.

It was on a clear, brilliant day in early August, 1813, that the anchor was weighed, sails set wide, and one vessel after another, the squadron sailed proudly out upon the waters of the lake ready to meet the British and engage with them.

But there was no enemy in sight. The British ships had vanished as completely as though they had never been there. For days they had been sailing up and down before the entrance to the creek, just out of gunshot, and seeming to taunt the American vessels and dare them to come out. And now they were gone. For three days Perry sailed up and down in search of the fleet. Then he learned where they were. They had sailed down to Malden, on the Detroit River, to gather more men and a fresh store of provisions, and also to wait there until a large new vessel, the *Detroit*, should be finished.

On the 9th of August Perry had a valuable reinforcement. Captain Elliott came from Buffalo to join him, bringing one hundred men. Perry at once put him in command of the *Niagara*, which was the largest vessel in the fleet except the flagship, the *Lawrence*. Each of these large vessels carried twenty guns. Of the other vessels in the squadron, three were so small that they only carried one gun each. The men and officers, all told, numbered about 400.

The British squadron had only six vessels, but they carried, all told, sixty-three guns, while the Americans had only fifty-four. They also had the advantage of being manned by trained and able seamen, many of whom had fought under Nelson.[4]

By September 1st Perry had become so impatient

to engage the British that he followed them down to Malden, but he found their squadron had drawn in close to the shore, where they were protected by the land batteries.

For a time Perry cruised up and down before them hoping to tempt them to come out from their shelter but they lay there quiet and motionless. At last he saw the uselessness of staying longer and sailed away and back to Put-in-Bay. This bay, thirty-four miles north of Malden, was the harbor he had chosen as the meeting-place for his vessels after cruises.

The 10th of September, 1813, dawned crisp and bright. A few scurries of rain in the early morning seemed only to clear the air. By ten o'clock the sun shone down from an almost cloudless sky and a light wind stirred among the rigging of the vessels.

Early in the morning Perry's squadron had sailed out from the harbor to the open water of the lake. All sails were set to catch the faint breeze. It was barely ten o'clock when a cry rang out from the lookout at the masthead of the *Lawrence:* "Sail ho!" and almost immediately followed the signals to the other vessels: "Enemy in sight," and "Get under way." Far off, down toward the mouth of the Detroit River, the sails of the British war-vessels could be seen white against the blue of the sky. They were coming at last.

The officers of the American squadron had already received written instructions from Perry as to the part they were to take in the battle. Now decks were cleared for action, and were sprinkled with water and covered with sand so that the men would not slip upon them. The gunners took their positions beside their guns.

On board the *Lawrence* Perry made a short address to his men. As he finished his address a great blue battleflag was unfurled and held up to view. On it, in white letters, were the dying words of the brave Captain Lawrence:

*"Don't Give Up The Ship!"*

"My brave lads," cried Perry, in a ringing voice, "this flag bears the last words of Captain Lawrence. Shall I hoist it?" A great shout went up from the men: "Ay, ay, sir! Ay, ay!" A moment later the blue flag was run up to the masthead. Cheer after cheer roared out across the water from every craft in the squadron. At the same time the wind caught the folds of the flag and blew it out so the words could be seen by all:

*"Don't Give Up The Ship!"*

It was Perry's message for the day. The wind was so light that though Perry's squadron moved on steadily it could make but slow progress. It was necessary for him to get close to the enemy's fleet, for the American guns had a much shorter range than those of the British. The British would be able to fire upon Perry's vessels long before they would be able to return the shots.

As the American fleet slowly drew on, Barclay's squadron ranged itself in a long line across the water. At the head of the line was the British flagship *Detroit*, with the small *Chippewa* close to her. Next to it came the *Hunter*. It was these two larger vessels and the *Queen Charlotte* that, a little later on, were to come near to destroying the *Lawrence*.

Aboard his flagship Perry paced up and down the deck. His face was quiet and serene, but his eyes were blazing with excitement. The officers were at their stations. Beside their guns lounged the gunners. The men were stripped naked to the waist, and about their heads they had knotted their handkerchiefs to keep their long hair out of their eyes. Many of them were veterans who had already fought on the famous *Constitution*.

Perry paused beside a group of them and looked from face to face. "I need not say anything to you," he said, "You know how to beat those fellows." The men grinned and their teeth showed between their parted lips. At a quarter to twelve the two flagships were still over a mile apart. The *Niagara* and some of the smaller American gunboats had fallen behind.

Then upon the *Detroit* a bugle was sounded. Its notes came faint but clear across the water. Immediately the British bands broke out with "Rule Brittania." There was a great cheer from the British, and a spurt of flame shot out from the side of the *Detroit*. Her long gun spoke out with a roar and a shot came bounding across the water toward the *Lawrence*. It fell short, but a few minutes later another shot, better aimed, crashed through the bow of the flagship.

The American gunners started to their places, but Perry lifted his hand. "Steady, boys, steady!" he cried. His vessels were still too far from the enemy for the guns to injure them.

The gunners sank back and the American squadron swept slowly on, without returning one of the shots that now began to pour hotly upon them splintering the masts, tearing the sails, and wounding the men.

Barclay had determined to direct his guns mainly at the *Lawrence.* If she could be destroyed, and her gallant commander with her, there would be little trouble in disposing of the rest of the fleet.

It was full ten minutes after the *Detroit's* first shot when a gun roared out from the American squadron. It was fired from the *Scorpion* by young Stephen Champlin, a cousin of Commodore Perry's. It was he, too, who was to fire the last shot in the engagement, as he had the first.

And now at last Perry gave the longed-for signal and his gunners sprang to their places. A moment later and their guns sent back a savage answer to the shots of the enemy. Several of the British ships were struck, but the American squadron had already been badly damaged while getting within reach of the enemy. The *Lawrence* had suffered most heavily, for, according to Barclay's plans, it was against her that their guns had been principally turned.

The *Detroit*, the *Hunter*, and the *Queen Charlotte* had gathered about her in a crescent and swept her with their shots. The *Niagara*, which was to have helped her by engaging the *Queen Charlotte*, still lagged far behind, almost out of gunshot. In a short time the spars and rigging of the *Lawrence* were carried away, her sails were in rags, her decks were wet with blood. So many men were injured that not enough were left to fire the guns. Many of the wounded men were carried down to the cockpit, but a shell crashing through killed a number of them.

A lieutenant who had come up to speak to Perry was struck and fatally wounded. A shot struck a hammock and drove it against Perry's young brother who stood beside him. The blow threw him across the deck, but he was unhurt.

Lieutenant Yarnell, fearfully wounded, but calm and cool, came to Perry, and told him every officer in his division had been killed. The Commodore gave him more men to fill their places. Presently Yarnell came back and told him that all these men, too, had been either killed or disabled. Perry had no more men to give him. "You must make out for yourself," he said. Without a word Yarnell went back to his place and began to aim and fire what guns he could with his own hands.

A seaman, black with smoke and powder, rushed up to Perry, crying wildly: "For God's sake give me more men!" but Perry had no more men to give him. Some of the wounded crawled up on deck to do what they could, but gun after gun fell silent.

The *Lawrence* was now little more than a floating wreck.

Some time before this Captain Perry had signalled to the *Niagara* to bring up the gunboats that were lagging behind. Captain Elliott passed the signal on to them, but he himself still hung back. It was not until after the last gun of the *Lawrence* had been silenced, and it might well be thought that her brave commander had been killed, that the *Niagara* got under way. Then her sails were set wide, and steadily she bore on toward the enemy.

Perry's heart rose with hope as he watched her approach. Then he saw she was not coming to the *Lawrence* at all. Unless she could be stopped she would pass it by.

The Commodore thought of a bold expedient.

He had a small boat lowered from the *Lawrence* and manned by a few stout oarsmen who were still left unwounded. Then the great blue battle flag was run down from the masthead. When the British saw the flag drop, they thought it was a sign of surrender, and cheer after cheer sounded from their vessels. Soon, however, they fell silent as they saw the stars and stripes were still left waving above the wreck of the flagship.[5] Wondering, they watched the *Lawrence*, trying to make out what it was that was happening aboard of her.

Suddenly out from under her bows shot the small boat. The sturdy rowers bent to their oars. Erect among them stood Commodore Perry. He was in full uniform and bore the battle flag in his hand. Its folds, wrapped about him, now floated out in the freshening wind. Beside him sat his little brother. He was crossing to the *Niagara* to take command of her.

So sure was he of reaching her in safety and of still winning the battle that he had changed his seaman's dress for a uniform, so as to be ready to receive the British officers when they came to surrender to him.

Between the flagship and the *Niagara* lay half a mile of open water. The air was heavy with smoke, and the sun shone through it on the water with a strange, unnatural light. All about towered the great, shattered, blackened battleships.

The small boat had hardly shot out into the open before the Commodore was recognized and the guns of all the British fleet were turned on that one small boat. Their mouths roared out, and shot and shell flew thick around it. An oar was shattered in a rower's hand. The salt water was dashed up in the oarsmen's faces till they were half blinded, but strangely enough no one was hurt. Just before Perry reached the *Niagara* a shot struck his boat, tearing a hole in the side. Instantly the Commodore tore off his coat and stuffed it in the hole, and so he kept the boat from sinking.

Fifteen minutes after leaving the *Lawrence* the Commodore sprang to the deck of the *Niagara*.[6]

He was met by Captain Elliott. "How goes the day?" he asked.

"Badly enough," answered Perry sternly; and then, "Why are the gunboats so far astern?"

"I'll bring them up," said Elliott.

"Do so," said Perry shortly.

Captain Elliott now took the Commodore's place in the small boat and started back toward the gunboats, while Perry made ready for a fresh attack upon the enemy.

With the coming of the *Niagara* the fortunes of the day were turned. Though the *Lawrence* had been almost shot to pieces, the British vessels themselves had been badly damaged. Perry had his seamen crowd on all the sail the *Niagara* could carry and bore down upon the enemy. The *Niagara* swept through the British line at full speed between the *Detroit*, *Queen Charlotte*, and *Hunter* on one side and the *Lady Provost* and *Chippewa* on the other. As she passed she poured out a deadly broadside.

The guns had been heavily loaded and she was so close to the enemy that every shot told.

As soon as she had passed through the line the *Niagara* was brought about and again poured out broadside after broadside.

The *Lady Provost* was almost cut to pieces.

The *Detroit* suffered heavily, while the other vessels were almost helpless against the heavy fire. Eight minutes after the *Niagara* cut through the line the British flagship lowered its flag in sign of surrender.

Cheer after cheer sounded from the decks of the American fleet. Even the wounded on the *Lawrence* joined in feebly. Standing there on the *Niagara* Perry caught off his cap, took out an old envelope, and resting it on the cap wrote in pencil this message:

"*We have met the enemy and they are ours — two ships, two brigs, one schooner, and one sloop. Yours with great respect and esteem, O. H. Perry.*" [7]

This dispatch was sent at once to General Harrison, who was in command of the American land forces. Perry then returned to the *Lawrence*, and it was to her ruined deck that the British officers came to make their surrender to her commander. Their looks were weary and sad. Many of them were wounded. Admiral Barclay was so badly hurt that he had to be helped on board. One after another they offered their swords to Perry, but one by one the swords were refused. His warm desire was to treat the enemy with all honor and courtesy.

The British deeply appreciated this generous behavior to them.

After they had left the *Lawrence* and returned to their own vessels, Perry threw himself down on the bare boards of the deck where he had been standing. He was so exhausted that he at once fell asleep and slept for some hours. All were careful that he should not be disturbed, but while he slept the news of the great victory he had won for our country was spreading everywhere. The newspapers of the day were filled with praises of his bravery, his daring, his nobility, and his generous behavior to the enemy, and it was then that he was given the title which has ever since been his:

*The Hero of Lake Erie.*

The Hero of Lake Erie

# NOTES

1. Oliver Hazard Perry was born at South Kingstown, Rhode Island, August 21, 1785.
His father was a naval officer and his four brothers were also trained in the service.

2. Presque Isle, now the town of Erie.

3. The construction of this fleet was under the charge of Sailing-Master Daniel Dobbins and Noah Brown, a shipwright of New York City.

4. The Lake Erie fleet consisted of the brig *Lawrence*, twenty guns; brig *Niagara*, twenty guns; brig *Caledonia*, three guns; schooner *Ariel*, four guns; schooner *Scorpion*, two guns and two swivels; sloop *Trippe*, one gun; schooner *Tigress*, one gun; schooner *Porcupine*, one gun.
In the British fleet were six vessels: the *Detroit*, nineteen guns and two howitzers; *Queen Charlotte*, seventeen guns and one howitzer; *Lady Provost*, thirteen guns and one howitzer; brig *Hunter*, ten guns; sloop *Little Belt*, three guns, and schooner *Chippewa*, one gun and two swivels.

5. Commodore Perry's dispatch to the Secretary of the Navy ran as follows: "U. S. Brig *Niagara*, off the Western Sister Head of Lake Erie, September 10, 1813, 4 p. m. Sir — It has pleased the Almighty to give to the arms of the United States a signal victory over their enemies on this lake. The British Squadron, consisting of two ships, two brigs, one schooner, and one sloop, have at this moment surrendered to the force under my command after a sharp conflict. I have the honor to be, sir, very respectfully,

"Your obedient servant,
"O. H. PERRY."

6. Perry left the *Lawrence* in charge of Yarnell. He was to hold out or surrender as he thought best. After consulting with the other officers who were left, Yarnell decided to haul down his flag. The vessel was only a helpless wreck, and the shots from the enemy were only causing greater suffering. When the wounded men in the cockpit heard what had been done they cried to Yarnell to sink the ship, that they might not fall into the hands of the British. This Yarnell refused to do. It was well that he did not, for scarcely more than half an hour later Perry returned to the flagship, and it was on her deck that the British officers came to make their surrender.

7. In a letter written to the Secretary of the Navy, Perry gives the following account of his taking command of the *Niagara*: "At half-past two, the wind springing up, Captain Elliott was enabled to bring his vessel, the *Niagara*, gallantly into close action; I immediately went on board of her, when he anticipated my wish by volunteering to bring the schooners, which had been kept astern by the lightness of the wind, into close action." There has been much discussion over this account, and it is felt by many to be a very generous attempt to make the best of the slowness of the *Niagara* and several of the gunboats in giving assistance to the *Lawrence*.

Rhode Island Boldly Refused to Sign

# How, Once Upon A Time, Rhode Island Bore Her Part In The Confederation

Brown University in 1776

IT WAS the year 1781, and all over the colonies there was the greatest joy and triumph. Bells were rung and cannon fired. For the war was almost over. Cornwallis had surrendered to Washington at Yorktown. The American colonies had won their independence from England, and the French had helped them, and everywhere in public places could be seen the crossed flags of France and America, with the British flag under them.

Down in Georgia and South Carolina the fighting was not yet entirely over. The British still held a few places there, but Greene and his forces were soon to drive them out. The Rhode Island troops were no longer needed in the North, so some of them were sent on down to join Greene, but the greater number came home to Rhode Island again.

Poor and gaunt and ragged these troops looked as they marched along the Rhode Island roads. Many of them were without hats or shoes. Some had nothing but cotton shirts and trousers to wear. The flags they carried had been almost shot to pieces on many a battlefield. But ragged and poor as they were, they laughed and joked on their way with all the cheerfulness that had made them the wonder of the French army.

To the Rhode Island people who waved their caps

to them and shouted and hurrahed these ragged soldiers seemed nothing less than heroes; they had been fighting for the freedom of the whole country.

But there was sorrow as well as rejoicing in the little state when the troops came marching home. Many a brave soldier would never come back. More than a third of the Rhode Island regiments had fallen on the battlefield or died of disease — smallpox or camp fevers. Even of those who returned many were maimed or crippled or sick.

The people at home had suffered as well as those who fought. Farms had been ruined and houses destroyed. There had been so little food in the state that many had almost died of starvation. Newport was ruined, its trees and orchards gone, its wharves destroyed, and many of its finest buildings burned. Bristol, Providence, Warren, and other towns had all suffered severely. Brown University had been closed to the students and used as a barracks and hospital. All trading had ceased. Even the ferries between the different towns had stopped running. While the British were there the people had been afraid to venture out on the water. They feared the guns of the British batteries and the British warships that lay just off the shore.

But now the British were gone. Their fortifications were deserted. The little Rhode Island children clambered about the earthworks and hunted for the bullets and cannon balls that had fallen there.

The ferries again plied between the towns. The business of the colony could once more be taken up, the farming, the fishing, and the trading. But it was hard to begin again when there was such poverty everywhere. The National Government itself was in need of money.[1] It could not even pay the soldiers who had fought for it. It called on the states to raise $8,000,000 for Government uses, for that was the very least that would be needed for the coming year of 1782. Rhode Island's share of this amount would be $216,000, but the little state was so poor that it was impossible for it to raise that much. It offered to pay a part of it with supplies for the army, but the Government would not agree to this.

In order to raise at least a part of the sum, fresh taxes were laid on the people of the little state; but already they had more than they could pay. In some cases, where the men had no money, the tax-collectors took their sheep and cattle from them to make up for the taxes they owed. This roused such a storm of ill-feeling, particularly in some of the Massachusetts towns, that in several places the people banded together to resist the collectors. They even attacked them and took away from them the cattle they had already seized.

Congress now proposed another plan for raising money for the Government. This plan was that each state should pay a tax or "impost" of 5 per cent. on all articles that were brought into it from foreign countries. Only a few articles were to be brought in free; of these a list was given. This plan was first proposed in 1781.

Eleven of the states agreed to it almost at once. Only Rhode Island and Georgia refused to consent.[2]

In 1777, while the war was still going on, the thirteen states had entered into a confederation, or "league of friendship," with each other. This confederation was for the sake of mutual help and strength against the enemy, and for "mutual and general welfare."[3]

In the Articles of Confederation that were written out for this league it was expressly said that each state was to keep its "sovereignty, freedom, and independence." Congress was to govern the general affairs of the league, but it was to have no right to control the trade of any state. Neither was it to have a right to levy a tax on the people of any state.

Rhode Island was very jealous of her liberty, the liberty that had been planned by Roger Williams and established by her charter. She would not have entered into the confederation at all unless she had been assured she would still be perfectly free in all state matters.

Now to give to Congress the right to tax her foreign trade was to change the Articles of Confederation. If money was to be raised in Rhode Island, her people claimed the right to raise it in their own way, and not by federal taxation.

Besides, Rhode Island was afraid that if this right were now given to Congress that body would soon claim other rights over the states as well. Before long they would find they were no longer free. So she was firm in her refusal to agree to it.

But this refusal blocked the whole matter, for the time at least. Naturally none of the other states wished to pay a tax unless all would, and the feeling in Congress against the little state was very bitter.

Rhode Island had still another reason for refusing to agree to the impost.

She carried on a larger foreign trade for her size than any other state. This meant that the imposts she would have to pay would be more than that of others.

The merchants of Rhode Island were already taking up their commerce again, and now their vessels journeyed farther than ever before. They had opened up a trade with China, and many new and beautiful and curious things were brought into the state from that country — silks, feathers, spices, preserved fruits, fans, quicksilver, window-screens, umbrellas — which were a great curiosity at that time — and many other things.

But there was another trade by which fortunes could be made more quickly and easily than by commerce with China. Before the war, when Newport was rich and prosperous, many of her wealthiest merchants made their money by buying and selling slaves. Now that they were poor it was no wonder they longed to take up the trade again.[4] Such large fortunes could be made in that way, and made so easily.

In 1774 Rhode Island had passed a law that no more slaves should be brought into the colony, but there were other places where the Newport traders could sell them — Georgia, the Carolinas, and other Southern States; so again their ships were bringing in cargoes of blacks that cost the shipowners little, and sold for high prices, and money was coming into Rhode Island for slave-traders at least, if for few others. In 1787 the assembly of the state passed a law forbidding *all* slave-trading, but even after that the business was still carried on secretly by many of her merchants.

Trading, fishing, and farming were not the only industries in Rhode Island, however. Their manufactures began to grow in number and importance, particularly in Providence. But the English were sending large quantities of their own manufactures into America, and were selling them more cheaply than Americans could afford to sell their own things.[5] Congress was still urging Rhode Island to agree to the impost, and at last, in 1785, she gave her consent. She gave her consent, however, not that the Government might raise money by it, but that her trade might be protected better than she could protect it herself.

Though the war had practically ended when Cornwallis surrendered at Yorktown, it was not until 1783 that a treaty of peace was signed between England and America. The first article in this treaty acknowledged the independence of the states.

When the treaty was received in America the states were once more filled with rejoicing. Once more cannon were fired and bells were rung. At Providence there was a procession, and sermons and addresses were given in the First Baptist Meetinghouse.

At high noon the proclamation was read from the balcony of the State House and other public places. Crowds gathered to hear it. There were shouts of joy; hats were tossed in the air, flags were waved, and military salutes were fired. A public dinner was given at the State House. The frigate *Alliance*, which had just returned from the West Indies, fired salutes, and all the shipping was decorated with flags. In the evening the town and harbor were illuminated, and fireworks were set off.

The rejoicings at Newport were no less than at Providence. A figure was made and dressed to represent Benedict Arnold, the traitor, and was burned by the Newport people with shouts and cheers.

Other towns all over the states celebrated with joy the proclamation of peace.

Our French allies had already left the country. They had sailed from Boston in 1782. On their way to that town they stopped at Providence for a time. The officers had been quartered in the houses there, and had been made as welcome as when they had stayed in Newport.

Brown University was now no longer needed as a hospital. It was once more opened to students, and in 1783 commencement exercises were held there, and five students were given the degree of Bachelor of Arts.

In that same year a very important law was passed in Rhode Island. It was a law that gave to Roman Catholics all the rights as citizens that other people had. These rights they had never had before.[6]

But there was another important act passed by the legislature that was to prove disastrous indeed to the little state, and that threw its people into distress and panic. There was so little ready money in the state, and it was so badly needed, that the legislature decided to issue paper money. A large amount of it was printed and sent out among the people.[7]

Many of the wisest people in the state were very much opposed to this issue of paper money, but the party that was in favor of it was the party that was in power. This paper money had no real value, as silver and gold have, or as much value as our own paper money has nowadays. There was but little gold or silver money in Rhode Island, yet great quantities of paper money were issued by the legislature. If the people had demanded gold and silver for the paper they held the state could not possibly have given it to them, and so all the paper money was worth little or nothing. No one outside of the state was willing to accept it. Even the Rhode Island dealers and merchants were very unwilling to give their goods for it. Many of them, indeed, refused to accept it, and would not sell their goods unless they were paid in silver or gold.

But the assembly was determined to make the people use it. It passed an act by which any one who refused to take the paper money when it was offered to him was to be fined $500; besides this, he was to lose his right to vote and all other rights as a freeman.[8]

The farmers and country people were, as a rule, very glad this act had been passed, for many of them had mortgaged their lands for this paper money. Now they could begin to use it, for no one would dare to refuse it.

So they came into the towns to pay their bills and buy goods with it. But rather than be forced into taking it the merchants closed their shops. Nothing could be bought.

To retaliate on the townspeople the farmers no longer brought their produce to the markets. If the tradesmen would not take their money, they should not have their goods, either, their butter and eggs, their vegetables, and poultry. Besides, the country people themselves had no wish to be paid for these things with still more paper money. Already they had more than enough.

The markets as well as the shops were closed. Trading ceased. Business came to a standstill. All over the state there was the greatest want and distress. People could not get enough to eat. In Newport there was a riot; a mob gathered and tried

# RHODE ISLAND IN THE CONFEDERATION

to force the grain merchants to give them corn for paper money. In Providence the town council borrowed five hundred dollars and sent outside the state to buy corn for the people. The distress was almost as great as in the war times, but now it was caused by the people of Rhode Island itself instead of by an outside country.

It was in May that the paper money party came into power, and forced their worthless paper upon the state. From that time on, for four months, the condition of Rhode Island became more and more miserable and the people grew poorer and poorer.

But in September, four months later, the matter was brought before the Supreme Court of Rhode Island. A Newport butcher had refused to accept paper money for his meat. When a fine was demanded from him, instead of paying he appealed to the court.

The court listened to the case, considered it, and gave as its decision that he need not pay the fine. It also decided that the assembly had no right to force people to accept paper money, or to lay a fine on them if they refused to do it.

As soon as the merchants and traders learned of this decision they were ready to take up business again. Shops were opened, produce was again brought to the markets, and the streets were filled with busy life. People were no longer afraid to offer their goods for sale since they would not have to take paper money; they could demand good gold and silver in exchange.

But while Rhode Island had been going through these times of panic and disaster the National Government had been considering a great and important matter. It was planning a close and more definite union among the states.

As long as the war with England lasted the states had been held together by their common danger as well as by friendliness. They all needed each other in their fight against the common enemy. But now that the war was over they found they needed a closer league than the Articles of Confederation gave them. It would be necessary to have a stronger central government, and to have some one to act as the head of the nation; not a king — the free states would never again submit to be ruled by a king—but a President who should be chosen by themselves, and should hold the position for a few years only.

More power must be given to Congress, too, and a court was appointed to decide quarrels or disagreements between the states. This court was to be called the Supreme Court. Whatever decisions it gave must be accepted by the states as final.

These three, Congress, the President, and the Supreme Court were to form the central government for the Union of States.

This plan of government was written out in a Constitution, and the states were asked to ratify the Constitution to show they agreed to it, and were willing to join the Union.

Delaware, the smallest state but one, was the first to ratify. One after another ten states followed the lead of Delaware. Only two, Rhode Island and North Carolina, were left. Of these North Carolina was undecided, but Rhode Island boldly refused to sign.

She declared (as she had once before declared about the impost) that this plan would interfere with her liberty.

When Rhode Island had refused to agree to the impost she had blocked the whole matter. But this Union of the States was a different affair. She might refuse to join, but she could not hinder the others from uniting. She would simply be left out, and this would place her in a dangerous position. She would be like a foreign state in the midst of another nation. She could neither hope nor demand their help in case she was in distress or danger.

Many people in the state realized all this. They were more than eager that Rhode Island should join the Union. But these were not the people who were in power. They could do little as long as the assembly was opposed to it. Vainly they urged and entreated the assembly to call a convention to consider the matter, and to talk it over. Again and again the assembly refused, or put them off with excuses.

In May of the year 1789 they sent a piteous petition. They wrote: "We have not an alliance or treaty of commerce with any nation on earth, we are utterly unable to defend ourselves against an enemy, we have no . . . protection or defence but from the United States of America." But even still, in spite of their appeals and arguments, no convention was called.

But Congress, which had been patient so long, now passed the first measure against the interests of Rhode Island. It declared that since Rhode Island had not joined the Union the time had come to treat her as a foreign power. Now all trade between her and the other states would be taxed, just as the commerce between America and England was.

This action of Congress threw Rhode Island into

204 ONCE UPON A TIME IN RHODE ISLAND

the greatest dismay and confusion. To place a duty on her trading meant ruin for her merchants and traders, and for the whole state. Eagerly she entreated Congress to wait, before passing this law, until she could again consider the matter of joining the Union.

Congress, unwilling to seem to use force with the little state, agreed to this. They agreed to wait until the 19th of January in the coming year, 1790.

But before that time Rhode Island had reconsidered the matter; she had changed her decision. She had agreed to accept the Constitution, and had entered into the Union of the United States of America.

In Providence and Newport the news of this decision was received with the greatest joy and relief. All over the state, indeed, the greatest satisfaction was shown. Rhode Island was saved. It was one of the Union, and at the next session of the Rhode Island Assembly, instead of closing, as always before, with the words "God save the state," the prayer now was "God save the United States of America."

Rhode Island was one of them.

The First Umbrella

# NOTES

1. By the time the Revolutionary War was ended the debt of the United States amounted to about seventy million dollars. Of this amount the Federal Government owed forty-five million; the rest was owed by the several states. England during the past seven years had doubled her national debt; it now amounted to two hundred and forty millions of pounds.

2. In this matter of refusing to agree to the impost Rhode Island was not so much alone as her detractors were fond of asserting. Few of the states were unanimous in their approval of the measure. Georgia never acted upon it, and Virginia presently repealed her grant. ("History of the State of Rhode Island and Providence Plantations.")

3. The Article of Confederation read: "A League of Friendship with each other for the common defence, the security of their liberties, and their mutual and general welfare."

4. The merchants of those days seemed to see there was very little difference between the negroes and any other salable merchandise. In a letter dated 1737, a certain Mr. Brown of Rhode Island wrote: "My Gineman (slave ship) is arrived. You may have a slave if you cum or send Befoar they are Gon." And in another letter he advises his brother, if he cannot sell his slaves to his mind, to bring some home. "I believe they will sell well. Get molasses or sugar. Make dispatch, for that is the life of trade."

5. England charged a high duty on all American goods sent into her markets.

6. "The most important act of this session (of the Assembly of 1783) . . . was a short statute extending to Roman Catholic citizens the same rights with the Protestants, thus repealing in effect the disabling clause (Catholics excepted) which had crept in no one knows how or when in the act which defined the requisites of citizenship." . . . "That a law excluding Roman Catholics as such would be a violation of the spirit of the charter, if not its letter also, all who read that instrument will admit." (Arnold's "History of the State of Rhode Island.")

7. "It must not be inferred that Rhode Island was alone in this matter . . . In the end only four of the thirteen states escaped the paper money craze." ("State of Rhode Island and Providence Plantations.")

8. The passage of this act was strongly opposed by Providence, Newport, Westerly, and Bristol. The Providence deputies entered a formal protest, but their protest was disregarded.

Made in the USA
Lexington, KY
18 July 2018